"(Cathy) created the Anthology as means of promoting and business owners around the world. (Her) expertise allowed us to bring our book, "The Anatomy of Accomplishment" from concept to the bookshelf. (Her) leadership allows women everywhere an opportunity to participate in the empowering world of entrepreneurship."

— Erin Joy,
Founder, CEO of Black Dress Circle®

"I was honored to be included with many other women who seek to help women become empowered. Through the guidance of Cathy and her staff, I got feedback that was helpful and encouraging. The process was effortless with the help of the editorial team. I loved the process and enjoyed meeting many other great authors who shared their stories to help others. Most of all, I am now a #1 international Best-selling author! What could be better than that?"

— Derlene Hirtz,
You Empowered Services

"I was excited to be part of a team that guided me every step of the way from initial idea brainstorming to promoting the finished book. The training, networking, and support did wonders for my confidence and allowed me to use the experience to share with my professional network."

— Mary Nunaley Co-Founder,
The Lavender Dragon Team, LLC

Clarity
OUT OF
CHAOS

Finding Our Way When
We Can't Always See the Path

Clarity Out of Chaos
Finding Your Way When We Can't Always See the Path
UPSI Daisy Press

Cover, Interior Design, and Project Management:
  Davis Creative Publishing Partners, CreativePublishingPartners.com

Writing Coach and Editor:
  Kay Uhles, KayClarkUhles.com

Compilation by Cathy L. Davis

Library of Congress Cataloging-in-Publication Data

Library of Congress Control Number: 2021920730

Clarity Out of Chaos: Finding Your Way When We Can't Always See the Path

ISBN: 978-1-7347971-7-6 (paperback)
        978-1-7347971-8-3 (ebook)

Page 107: NIV, New International Version

▲ ▲ ▲

To the Dreamers and Imagineers
who became their own light and
found their way through the mist.

▲ ▲ ▲

The Chaos of an Unconscious Mind

uncountable
unsortable, a mangle of
words, images clamoring
demanding immediate attention
the repetitive notes of an annoying tune
names not quite remembered
shrapnel from exploded dreams
they push and shove,
crowded in a space with no dimension
caught in that singular span of time
before limbs stiff from all-night poses stretch
and pressure shifts off aching shoulders
knees and hips
just
before
the eyelids lift
then it's all so swift, chaos swept away
relegated to the dark
unfinished realm, waiting to be sorted
organized and gathered into
calm, clear, actionable thoughts–
it's good to be awake.

– Cheryl Roberts
October 9, 2021

TABLE OF CONTENTS

Rollin' With Life

Cathy L. Davis

I've never been a big fan of roller-coaster rides—be that literally or as a metaphor for business or in life. A *little* excitement is good, but…

I remember, as a young, pre-school child sitting in the back seat of the family car (WAY before seatbelts—let alone car seats—were required). The gravel country road to my grandmother's house was a bit hilly. It was a game for me and my mother, the driver, to see if she could "wake up the butterflies" in my tummy. On that rocky road, if my mother accelerated just a bit before she approached the crest of a hill, the car would slightly elevate off the ground. It would feel as if we were flying and the butterflies in my tummy would "flutter"! As a three- and four-year-old, not yet tall enough to see out the window, it was fun and exciting. When I later drove that same road as an adult, with a new, adult perspective, I realized how much of a daredevil my mother really was. And that road was NOT just "a bit hilly." There was NO WAY (in H-E-DOUBLE-L) I was going to accelerate over those hills (let alone on gravel) to a speed that would recreate those childhood "butterflies" in my tummy. Was she CRAZY?! Apparently, she had a secret desire to be a racecar driver.

Life is all about perspective…and roller coasters

In life, one day when we least expect it, we wake up without a job or divorced or having some unknown virus…or sitting on something called "Space Mountain" at Disney World (which is the LAST roller coaster anyone convinced me to ride).

Life has its way of giving us a ride… known as "life lessons." I've learned it's not necessarily the "WHAT" that gets tossed our way that is the lesson, but the "HOW" we react to it that is our true education. If we live long enough, we will certainly encounter a hilly pathway, our proverbial bumps in the road. We each get the choice to ride through the lessons however we want. It's our choice whether to accelerate and turn those bumps into a wild ride of excitement with butterflies in our tummy or to choose to slow down, reflect, ponder a bit…then approach those bumps/hills/mountains with a calculated, well-thought-out, step-by-step process.

Rollin' with life

It was dark and I was cold. I could see the flashing lights all around me as we sped through curves and over mountains. My heart was racing, and my grip on the rail in front of me was frozen tight. I closed my eyes, bounced in my seat, and held on for dear life. I prayed to not fall out and for the ride to be over quickly so life could get back to normal.

Then, I heard a man's voice… "Cathy, you have to let go of the rail and stand up."

I opened my eyes to see a friendly face extending his hand to help me up. I was the last one left on the roller coaster. My legs were cramping and wobbly at the same time. I was experiencing that feeling you get when your hand goes to sleep and you're afraid to move it even though you can't feel a thing. I didn't know whether I should hug him or cry. I had SURVIVED Space Mountain!

The lessons are not lost on me here. There are times I approach a bump in the road of life much like my mother—full speed ahead!—and other times when I close my eyes, hold on tight, and hope for the best. The latter is when I've learned to look for that friendly face with the extended hand to grab onto. I've also learned to be the one who extends the hand.

These are not just stories…these are the voices of experience

The stories you'll read in this collection of essays, *Clarity Out of Chaos,* hold many lessons for each of the authors. The one lesson they collectively share is that LIFE is a roller coaster and the hard times are not necessarily there to break a person—they can also make a person. The tough times show us our resilience, our tenacity, our creative ability for problem-solving. Our confidence is born out of these rough, difficult times because, once we get to the other side of the chaos, we rise and move forward with a greater perspective and clarity.

And I was quite clear when I got off that Space Mountain ride, I was never getting on another roller coaster again.

Cathy L. Davis is Founder/CEO Davis Creative Publishing Partners. She is a Creative Publishing Consultant, Designer, Imagineer, and Multiple #1 Amazon International Bestselling Author.

Books are in Cathy's DNA and have always played a big role in her life. Cathy Davis believes we all have a story to tell, and it is through our stories that we find our voice, share our wisdom, and make a difference in the lives of others. After all, wisdom not shared is wisdom lost forever.

Cathy founded Davis Creative, LLC in January of 2004 after spending the bulk of her corporate career as a Designer and Creative Director at Bank of America's Trust Division, managing a team of designers and print specialists. What originally began as a boutique creative services agency, is now known as Davis Creative Publishing Partners, a sought-after publishing industry leader, providing concierge publishing services for quality-conscious authors around the corner and around the world.

cathy@daviscreative.com
https://creativepublishingpartners.com
https://www.linkedin.com/in/cathyldavis/
https://www.youtube.com/channel/UC5L1yOYzT0gPP-tXY02ltVA
https://www.facebook.com/DavisCreativeLLC
https://www.instagram.com/cathyl.davis/

An Eagle's Vision

Marian McCord

My life seemed perfect. I was living the American dream, with a great husband, three amazing children—fourteen, eighteen, and twenty-two years old—and a four-legged fur-baby! I worked as a pediatric nurse. Track meets, soccer, homework, and college visits filled our days, as did laughter, friends, and fun! Despite our busy lives, we found time to gather together for worship, dinner, and ice cream!

In September 2003, my life changed. My middle son, Chad's girlfriend called me. Chad—a gifted high school student, athlete, youth group leader, equestrian-therapy-for-children volunteer, with twenty college credits, and a Division I college soccer coach pursuing him—had a promising future.

"Mrs. McCord," she said, "Chad needs to talk to you. Is it okay if I come over?"

Thirty minutes later, my life changed forever.

"I want to end my life. I have been thinking about it for a long time."

My heart sank. My stomach was tied in knots. I replied as a good pediatric nurse would.

"Chad, it sounds like you might have depression. Depression is treatable and there is help. Will you be safe tonight?" He assured me he would.

Chad slept. I did not!

I scheduled an appointment with a child psychiatrist, to whom Chad had disclosed that he had been thinking about taking his life since third grade and that he knew his life's journey would end his senior year of high school.

I had no idea he was depressed. How did I miss this?

On that first doctor visit, we were encouraged not to discuss Chad's college plans, as Chad felt he would not be able to stop the suicidal thoughts once he left home to live on campus. For the first time in Chad's life, he began taking anti-depressants. He was embarrassed and asked us not to tell his brother or anyone about his depression, seeing a psychiatrist, and taking medication.

Eight days after our initial conversation about his suicidal thoughts, flashing lights of emergency vehicles outside our home demonstrated how sick Chad was. Chad was checked and treated by paramedics while he lay unconscious on the bathroom floor. I screamed. I cried. I shook. How could this have happened to him, to my family?

Our journey through the mental health system began with intensity beyond my wildest imagination. Over the next six months, the journey escalated with more worry, fear, and concern for Chad. I intervened on four of his six suicide attempts; his eighth-grade brother intervened on the fifth; the hospital staff, on the sixth. Each attempt resulted in another hospital admission, new medications, and eventually electroconvulsive therapy (ECT). On each admission, Chad was stripped of personal belongings and hopes of a recovery. Nothing was helping. Unlike Chad, I was able to grab onto hope, support, and understanding offered by many. Our family was on guard 24/7. We couldn't leave Chad alone. Between suicide attempts and hospitalizations, Chad completed his schoolwork at home, played basketball with his brother, and finished his Eagle Scout project. Concentrating was difficult, frustrating.

He said, "Mom, I cannot think like I used to. It is hard to concentrate. I don't have anything to give the world anymore."

I celebrated the mini breakthroughs and reprieves, such as the first few days after an ECT treatment. But relief would be short-lived, as he cycled back into his depression each time. Chad leaned into his old humorous self, occasionally, when the veil of depression temporarily lifted. It gave me hope. Knowing he would cycle back into his depression, Chad joked, "I guess, I just can't hold my charge."

Despite cognitive deficits caused by ECT, Chad found the courage to finish the oral Eagle Scout test; he earned the highest rank of a Boy Scout. A proud moment for all of us!

His suffering was intense; his recovery, obscure. I thought, *If only he could have gotten cancer instead of his mental illness.* To think that as an oncology nurse and mom speaks volumes of the devastation of his illness.

I longed for successful treatment, resources, and a compassionate mental health system. It was not to be found. Hospital beds and research focused only on children's physical ailments—so unfair and wrong! How could our health system treat children with mental-health challenges so differently than kids with cancer? It made no sense! We deserved better!

Soon, all hope faded for Chad.

During a drive to one of his therapy sessions, he said, "Mom, I know it is going to be hard on you when I am gone, but you will get used to it, and your life will be better without me."

I assured him, my life would never be the same without him and asked him to stay in the fight. I acknowledged how hard it was and explained that the doctors needed more time to try other treatments. But deep inside, I was losing hope too. I prayed.

On April 15, 2004, I encouraged Chad to get some exercise.

"That is not a good idea," he said, playing a computer game—or so I thought. Actually, he was writing a suicide note to his girlfriend.

Later, he said, "I am ready to run now."

We ventured off to our church's soccer fields. I watched him run and was excited to see he had found his beautiful running stride, which I had not seen for months. I thought, *His head, heart, and feet are connected. Praise God, he has turned the corner!* If only that was the case! Ten minutes later, my son was dead by suicide.

I was numb, in shock. I cried and paced back and forth, running my hands through my hair. My life, my family, my dreams—shattered.

A parent's love for their children is beyond expression. A part of me died that day with Chad. I wanted to crawl into the grave with him. Grief and guilt tormented me. I could not eat or sleep. I questioned my role in his suicide. How did I fail him as his mother? Why didn't I know and recognize the warning signs?

Chad's death set me on a journey I was ill-prepared to make. How would I push through? I reflect now on those choices and decisions I needed to make: anger versus acceptance, despair versus hope, silence versus openness. I sought counseling and allowed family and friends to hold me up. I focused on acceptance, hopefulness, and openness, and developed a burning desire to make a difference for kids like Chad. It gave me strength and purpose.

Several months before his death, Chad sat crossed-legged on his hospital bed. He shared his vision. "When I get better—and I know I am not there yet—I want to go back to my school and say, 'My name is Chad McCord and I have depression.' I want to teach other kids not to do what I did, which was to hide my illness in shame and silence."

Chad will never be able to fulfill his vision, but as his parents we have vowed to be his voice. And CHADS—an acronym for Communities Healing Adolescent Depression and Suicide—Coalition for Mental Health was born. CHADS' mission is to save young lives by advancing the awareness and prevention of depression and suicide.

Today, I wish all parents…

- ▲ knew the warning signs of depression and suicide.
- ▲ knew the importance of seeking professional help.
- ▲ knew how to talk to their kids about anxiety, depression, and suicide.
- ▲ listened, nonjudgmentally, and kids felt safe talking with their parents or a trusted adult about their mental health.
- ▲ knew that suicide is the second leading cause of death for ten- to twenty-four-year-olds.

From our dining table—the table where fun family dinners with Chad took place—CHADS Coalition took shape and grew beyond our kitchen walls to an organization with a $2,000,000 budget and forty-five people. CHADS is now one of the largest providers of suicide prevention for middle and high school students in the country. Through CHADS' Signs of Suicide Program, we work with 60,000 (and counting) young people a year in all but one St. Louis Metro area school district. Forty-seven percent of the 600 students we counsel every year are suicidal. Giving kids, parents, and school staff tools to discuss mental health and the resources to get help when needed is critical. CHADS' Family Support Program provides compassionate clinical support, focusing on each child's strengths! Lastly, CHADS' Social and Emotional Wellbeing Mentoring Program works with kids struggling with social and emotional skills, reducing trips to the principal's office by forty-two percent.

Chad lit the burning fire in my heart to help kids live happy, healthy lives. In memory of him, my husband and I devote our lives to youth suicide prevention. Our wish is that our story will never be your story!

In 2004, after losing her 18-year old son Chad to suicide, Marian transitioned her career from saving lives in the hospital to saving lives in the community. She and her husband co-founded CHADS Coalition for Mental Health. CHADS is an acronym for Communities Healing Adolescent Depression and Suicide. CHADS mission is to save young lives by advancing the awareness and prevention of depression and suicide.

It was Chad's dream that after he got better, he would go back to his school and teach kids not to do what he did which was to hide his illness in shame and silence. After his death, Marian vowed to be his voice of hope to raise awareness about teen depression and suicide.

As Executive Director, she now leads one of the largest school based suicide prevention agencies in the country. She looks forward to bringing CHADS services to schools throughout Missouri.

www.chadscoalition.org
https://www.facebook.com/chadscoalition
https://www.instagram.com/chadscoalition
https://www.linkedin.com/in/marian-mccord-745b06196
314-952-2046

Clarity, Order, and Beauty Out of Chaos

Theresa Jeevanjee, Ph.D.

Chaos. When most people think of chaos, they think of frenzy, disorder, and confusion. In fact, those concepts pretty well define the word according to online searches I've made. "Chaotic" describes often out-of-control and unpredictable situations. A good example may be the 2020 pandemic and its results.

In physics "chaos" describes behavior that is so unpredictable it appears random; it is very sensitive to small changes in conditions. A branch of mathematics called "chaos theory" deals with fractals, beautiful pictures of chaos. More on that later, and I promise not to get "too math-y."

In some sense, my life has been chaotic since my son, Ryan, was born. Ryan has a rare chromosome disorder, which manifests in mental and physical disabilities. He is also a rare gift. Ryan's birth started me on a journey that is best described as chaotic—a journey certainly made more chaotic by the pandemic.

There are times in life we all will remember forever. The kind of moments that, no matter where we are, we can close our eyes and relive them: the death of President Kennedy; the destruction of the twin towers; the births of our children…and the announcement of the lockdown due to a world-wide pandemic.

In my family, increased chaos started months before the lockdown. My husband, Zulfi, had worked at the same company for over fifteen years. He was unhappy but comfortable and well-paid. He had looked for a new job on and off for years; finally, one with potential arose. Problem was, it was in Chicago.

We have lived in St. Louis for over thirty years and have raised our three children, Ryan, Kiran, and Lauren, here. We have a strong community of caregivers and medical providers for Ryan, and we have a lot of friends. Logistically, moving to Chicago would not be easy. So we decided Zulfi would commute to and from Chicago for a year to try it. Ryan and I would join him later.

At the time, I was teaching at the all-girls high school where our two daughters had graduated. Teaching there brought a fair amount of chaos in its own right—I also helped with the robotics team. My days and nights were very long. Living and caring for Ryan alone, with Zulfi in Chicago, proved to be quite challenging.

On top of being alone that year, I caught every virus the students carried into the school, including whooping cough and bronchitis—*at the same time.* One day, I awoke in the very early morning unable to breathe. I cannot remember a time when I felt so frightened and helpless.

Zulfi was in Chicago; Kiran and Lauren were away at college; and Ryan was sleeping in his room. I managed to call 911. At some point my airway cleared enough to cough out that I could not breathe. I suppose that was obvious because they said they had already sent an ambulance. By the time the ambulance got there, I was breathing again—although my breaths were more like gasps—and coughing a lot, too.

I have a new respect for people who need inhalers. I could never be away from mine. It took me months to recover. During those months, I discerned I needed to work somewhere else, preferably a university. Perhaps going to Chicago would not be so bad.

In the meantime, I had lots of help at home with Ryan, and I settled into a groove at the high school. I did not mind being by myself and loved being with Ryan, so it was not too bad for me. I interviewed for and was offered a position at a university during that time, so I was actually pretty hopeful. But the commute and transition to his new job was harder on Zulfi than we had expected.

I have a strong faith and a deep spiritual life, which helped get me through my own chaotic journey in those days without my husband to help. My faith deepened.

Zulfi has always supported my faith. He believes in God but lacks respect for "man-made religions." I get that. He usually comes to mass with me, but

I know he does not believe in much of it. And that is okay. It is his journey, and I am happy to be a part of it.

Knowing how intelligent Zulfi is and how hard he works, I believed, predicted, and prayed that his new challenges would result in one of two things: (1) Either he would succeed at his new company in Chicago or (2) the job would provide a path to something better. I knew it deep down. I also prayed that the commute might get easier and for the best possible outcome.

In March 2020, although I did not have the clarity to see it then, the answer to my prayers had begun. Because 20/20 vision is very good, many have commented on the irony of the year 2020 being so murky. And murky it was in so many ways. By 2020, I was in my second semester at my new university position. The first couple of years as a professor at a new place are always challenging, but I was happy anyway.

Throughout my career as a teacher and during the girls' education, it was rare that our spring breaks ever coincided. But in 2020 they did. And the extension of spring breaks, to "flatten the curve" of the pandemic, at our three universities coincided, too. The girls came home for an extended break with just enough clothes—we were told two weeks. Zulfi came home from Chicago, too, welcoming two weeks without commuting. Then we got the announcement that no one would be returning because of the pandemic, and we were thrust into online teaching and learning and working from home.

To say that going from home alone with Ryan to having everyone back and competing for internet and other resources was chaotic is a huge understatement. But I was grateful they were all well, that we had a large home, and that we always had enough to eat.

Zulfi eventually adjusted to working from home and became happy about the situation, especially not commuting. He went from "the quiet new guy" in the Chicago office to making a difference for the company from home. We were all adjusting to our new situation—or were certainly trying.

Online college classes, teaching for me and learning for the girls, proved tough. The girls missed their friends and being in class in person. While I was happy not to have my thirty-minute-plus commute, I missed seeing my students and colleagues. Interacting with students is the most nourishing part of my job.

Not seeing their faces or being able to get to know them was hard. And online teaching brought about issues I had never expected. By the time we started the next semester "fully virtual," I had four classrooms full of students, the vast majority of whom I had not met.

Most classroom teachers have dealt with cheating throughout their careers, but it increased, for me, at least ten-fold after converting to online. Because online teaching took so much more time and effort, I thought, *I am working so hard, and some students respond by cheating?!*

I teach mostly computer science, but I had one class called "Applied Discrete Mathematics," which is considered very challenging. I have taught it several times and really like it. I tease the kids, "It's okay if you do not like it. I like it enough for all of us."

I spent about three weeks on a concept called "sum of products." The sum represents a computer "OR gate" and the product an "AND gate." Applying the method of sum of products is an important part of minimizing circuits and helps achieve the smallest possible computing device. In case none of that makes sense, the only thing to understand at this point is that the sum of products is abbreviated "SOP."

After three weeks going over the concept, for the first test on the subject, I asked, "What does 'SOP' stand for; give an example of how to apply it." Five students answered "standard operating procedures" and gave military tactical examples—the first thing that comes up in a Google search for "SOP."

What?!

When I asked whether I should report it, I was told probably not because I did not specify the students could not search Google and did not ask "What is SOP in *this class*?" It may sound funny now, but at the time it was not.

To make matters worse, because the students had signed up for an in-person class that was converted to online, we could not require cameras or proctoring during testing. It became clear I needed to spend more time crafting "Google-proof" assessments and writing more specific instructions. I was already working eighty-plus hours a week!

During the 2020 pandemic lockdown, local and state governments imposed restrictions on gatherings. Our family had many milestones during that time:

Ryan's thirtieth birthday, Lauren's twenty-first, my sixtieth, Kiran's and Lauren's graduations, and Zulfi and my twenty-fifth wedding anniversary. I had planned to have a big party to celebrate these milestones with carriage rides. Instead, we got creative. For example, for my birthday, the girls and Zulfi planned a neighborhood parade led by police friends; they arranged a video chat with extended family and friends and spoiled me all day. I will always remember my sixtieth as one of the most special days of my life. Rather than what I missed due to the pandemic, I focused on what I had.

Lockdown also created confusion for Ryan. He did not understand why he was not allowed to do his regular activities. Masses were offered online, but Ryan and I went to church early and sat quietly, as we had done before the pandemic. Father Kevin would come say hi, which Ryan loved. Then we would go home and watch mass online, where Ryan would try to say hi to Father Kevin thinking it was a video chat and not a recording. That created more confusion, but it was very sweet and always made me smile.

All through the pandemic, we tried to focus on the positive. We took turns cooking and made lovely meals at home. We discovered good restaurants that delivered. And with all the people we knew who had it much worse—some who paid the ultimate price of death—I focused on gratitude.

In the middle of the chaos, Zulfi received a recruiting call for a Fortune 5 company in pharmaceuticals and healthcare. He had never talked about work being a vocation before, but I said, "Wouldn't it be great if you could apply what you know to making drugs and health care less expensive." And after much discussion and discernment, he used the word "vocation" when he resigned from his Chicago job. Both of my predications had come true: (1) He succeeded where he was and (2) the job had helped him learn what he needed for something better: his new pharmaceuticals/health-care job—or, rather, his new *vocation*.

Seeing good outcomes, beauty and order, is difficult when we are thrust into chaotic situations. What my family experienced through the pandemic reminds me of the relationship between chaos theory and fractals. Fractals, again, are the visual identity of chaos, truly beautiful representations of infinite, recursive formulas and seemingly random systems. They are prevalent in nature.

To see chaos turned to beauty, search for "images of fractals" on Google, also "Where Math, Nature, and Art Meet" (http://ifsa.my/articles/fractals-where-math-nature-and-art-meets) to see explanations of images like below:

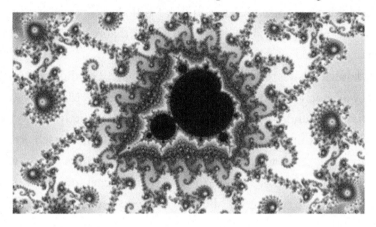

No matter what definition of chaos you use, aspects of the infinite—or at least seemingly infinite—exist. Chaos seems random. Chaos is sensitive to small changes and can be hard to navigate. But just as fractals are the orderly and beautiful pictures of chaos, faith (along with hard work and attitude adjustment) can bring clarity, order, and beauty to any chaotic life situation.

Dr. Theresa Jeevanjee teaches computer science and mathematics at Lindenwood University and for MEGSSS (Mathematics Education for Gifted Secondary School Students). She enjoys running, painting, cooking, and taking ballet classes.

Theresa is an associate in the CSJ (Congregation of St. Joseph) community and is active in two prayer groups. Her volunteer work includes tutoring mathematics, helping with the theatre and chorus costumes for her daughters' former high school, and helping her neighborhood and parish.

Theresa and her husband live in Webster Groves, Missouri, with their children, Ryan, Kiran, Lauren, and their dog, Kuki Monster.

Theresa can be reached at:
tjeevanjee@gmail.com
faithandrelentlesslove.com

Respect Your Art

Kim Pearson

My high school art teacher, Mr. J, never sugar-coated his praise or his criticism. He didn't like me. This was unusual because all my teachers had always liked me. I was an A student and always turned in my homework on time. This was not because I was a brown-nose. I found schoolwork pretty easy.

Art was easy for me too. I had a good sense of color and design; I could capture likenesses. So I just didn't understand why Mr. J didn't like me. With the other students, he would laugh and joke around, or he would discuss art with them and treat their opinions with respect. With me, he said little and what he said seemed to be encased in ice. My projects always came back graded "B" with no comments.

At the beginning of my junior year, Mr. J gave us a year-long assignment. We were to create something—anything—a painting, sculpture, drawing, or whatever we wanted, using any kind of media we chose. This "something" was to express what was unique and original about us. "Why were you born?" said Mr. J. "Your project should answer that question."

I don't think Mr. J truly expected a bunch of sixteen-year-olds to produce works of great originality or beauty or come remotely close to answering his grandiose question. But that was no reason not to ask it.

Because I was a quick study and easily mastered school subjects, I had developed a bad habit: procrastination. So I didn't start work on the year-long project until just a couple of weeks before it was due. I didn't even think about it. How hard could it be?

When I did begin the project, I still wasn't thinking about it much. One day as I was doing algebra homework at a friend's house, gossiping and giggling as we "worked," I kept us amused by doodling along the sides of my paper. My doodles were quick sketches of my friend's new kitten. The kitten was a striped creature full of mischief and grace, and my doodles must have caught some of her goofy spirit for it leaped off the page. The kitten gamboled, she sneered, she preened, she looked wise, and most of all she looked very funny. My friend went into transports of delight over the doodles, and I was proud of (and secretly surprised by) how good they were. Good enough for even Mr. J to be impressed by them.

So I decided that my kitten doodles would be my year's project. But since I couldn't submit them on the margins of an algebra paper, I had to come up with another media. The obvious choice was pen-and-ink drawing, but I felt that wasn't original enough. Earlier, I had become interested in the art of tapestry, although all I'd done was look and admire—I'd never tried any kind of needlework. But how hard could it be?

I got my mother to take me to the fabric store to buy yarn and needlepoint canvas. I didn't pay any attention to the different kinds of canvas; I just bought what I thought looked right. I paid the same lack of attention to the different kinds of yarn and needles available; I got the yarn in colors that "called" to me, and a needle was a needle, right? I didn't buy a frame to hold the canvas or any instructions on how to block it. I didn't see why that should be necessary.

When I got my tools home, I cut the canvas up into six different squares, for my six different kitten poses. The edges of the canvas were a little rough and uneven and starting to fray already, but I'd fix that later, I thought. I transferred my sketches to the nubbly canvas—it was harder than I expected, but the kittens still looked goofy and mysteriously graceful. Then I started to stitch. I didn't read anything about different kinds of needlepoint stitches, I just began pushing my needle in one hole and out another. I mean, how hard could it be?

Hard. Really hard. I must have stitched those six kittens at least twenty times each, trying to turn that intractable yarn into sneers and whiskers, grace and mischief. Every spare minute I had I spent working on those kittens, as the due date came closer and closer.

Well, I learned tapestry-making the hard way, but I did learn. When the tapestries were finished, the night before they were due, the needlepoint kittens were even better than the original doodles, and I knew I had created something truly magical. The only problem was that I had no time left to "fix" the frayed and ragged edges; and since the canvas had not been stretched at the beginning, some of my kittens had begun to droop in the middle. And the only way to fix that would be to start all over.

They'd have to do as they were, but I was not that worried—I knew how good those kittens were. My artist's eye told me so.

When it was my turn in class to display my project, I thumbtacked the kitten canvases up on the wall. I could hear some of the students saying complimentary things, like "Those are so cool!"

Mr. J, however, said nothing. He just looked at the kittens for a long time. Finally, he turned to me to deliver his verdict.

"You fulfilled this assignment perfectly," he began. "Your piece does express what is unique about you. And it makes me furious.

"These could have been the best art I've seen from a high-school student," he continued. "Those kittens are original and beautiful and make us want to laugh with joy. They make us want to keep looking at them—until we see the sloppy technique and lazy presentation that you have chosen for them. Here's what I see now when I look at them—I see an artist who does not respect her art or her talent. I see someone who does not have the courage to live up to her gifts. I no longer want to laugh at your kittens; now I want to cry."

And with that, he walked out of the room, slamming the door behind him, leaving us all—especially me—stunned.

This memory from a long time ago makes me cringe when it pops up, as it still does sometimes, whenever I have an attack of arrogance or the lazies.

Maybe Mr. J was too harsh with me; after all, I was only sixteen. But I don't think so.

By dismantling my arrogance and forcing me to face the truth, Mr. J nipped tendencies in the bud that could have crippled me all my life. I am eternally grateful that he didn't like me. He respected my art even when I didn't, and that was enough.

Kim Pearson is a writer, artist, poet, and memoirist. She is the author of over a dozen books, which include fiction, non-fiction, memoirs, children's books, and poetry. Her latest book is "The Masks on Grandmother's Wall," both written and illustrated by her. Kim has also ghostwritten many books for others, many of which are memoirs. She teaches memoir writing to senior citizen centers and other groups, because she believes that everyone has a story and that all of us are part of history.

For more information about Kim, visit her website www.kimpearson.me.

Clarity in the Chaos:
A Glimpse of Heaven

Diane Finnestead, MAT, Ed.S.

March 11, 2021. I boarded the plane from St. Louis to Charleston. When I landed, the world had changed forever by a "worldwide pandemic." Fear of the unknown set in as I waited for my long-distance boyfriend of two years to greet me at baggage.

After the hug and kiss, I asked, "Did you hear the news?"

He said in his southern drawl, "Yep, what you worried about, Honey?"

"I'm worried about not getting back home to St. Louis. I only packed for three days...how long can I stay?"

Without hesitation, he took my hand, "You can stay here with me forever."

With that, my eyes welled up with tears; and as we walked to the car, I tried to get my emotions in check. I kept thinking, *I can't go into a pandemic all ooey-gooey*, so I focused on what I'd read every day for years, a cross-stitch my sister had made: "Put on your Big Girl pants and deal with it!" Ah-ha!

I took a deep breath and put my "big girl pants on" as I got in my man's truck. The statements "Life happens" and "Attitude is everything" consumed me as my sweetheart asked me why I was so quiet on the car ride back to his home from the airport. I told him that I was trying to gain some clarity in the chaos of the day's events and wondered how this news could affect us and those we love.

My thoughts were racing from *For God's sake, this was supposed to be the twentieth celebration of my thirtieth birthday* (because it doesn't sound sexy to say "fiftieth birthday"), *a three-day weekend at the beach in Charleston with the man I love*, to *I forgot to pack underpants*, to *Thank heaven I remembered to put swimsuits in my weekender bag,* to *Every well-visited American beach town has a Wal-Mart close by if I forgot to bring something—like underwear!* Honestly, to deal with a pandemic, where does one find big girl pants big enough?

I continued in my out-loud voice to explain that I needed to draw from unrelated past experiences to realize the wisdom that might have prepared us for this day and the days ahead.

"Make sure you impart anything profound or funny that bubbles up," he requested while smiling and winking at me.

And over the next few days as we watched the television—too much— I shared three stories that would help me cope and find clarity through the next seventeen months, until I was fully vaccinated and could return to St. Louis. These three stories taught me what I needed to do to survive the pandemic.

Be Yourself

I was just a wee one when my Aunt Diane came all the way from Wyoming to visit St. Louis for the first time. My mom picked her up at the airport and headed down to Laclede's Landing by the Arch to get a beer in the historic part of St. Louis. My mom headed to the restroom. Aunt Di was sitting at the bar, alone, when a gentleman came over in a Budweiser jacket and asked if he could buy her a beer. My Aunt replied, "No, I already have one. I have a Coors."

To which this gentleman replied, "You sure you don't want a Bud? You are in Budweiser country."

And Aunt Di said, "Okay, I'll take another beer. You can get me another Coors."

Then he asked her where she was from and what she did for a living.

"Originally from Nebraska, now a principal at a school in Wyoming, here visiting my sister for the first time." Then she asked, "What do you do?"

Aunt Di turned around to see my mom returning and noticed a group of guys in Budweiser jackets carrying a cake. The gentleman pointed saying, "I'm with those guys. We're celebrating a win today. I'm with the Budweiser Racing Team."

Aunt Diane proclaimed, "I didn't know they raced the Clydesdales!"

I love my Aunt Diane. May she rest in peace.

What this story taught me during the pandemic chaos was to be myself no matter where I am or what life throws at me. Some say when in Rome, do as the Romans do; I say, wherever you are, be you. Go with the flow. Don't try to be someone you are not. In the words of Shakespeare, "First to thine own self be true." Be true to what you want and who you are and always leave room to not take yourself so seriously. Laugh when you say something ridiculous—that's what Aunt Di did, and now generations of our family have shared this story. Be yourself.

Be Flexible

My buddy since age three was getting married about twenty-five years ago. He came over to visit. His parents were divorced and he'd known my mom and dad his entire life. Mom and I were sitting in the kitchen. The windows to the back porch were open. We began to hear a very serious conversation ensue between my buddy and my dad. My buddy, inquisitive about marriage in general due to his upcoming nuptials, asked my dad (Rodger) about being married to my mom (Jayne). At the time, my mom and dad had been married for twenty-five years.

My friend asked, "Rodger, how have you been able to stay married for all these years?"

My dad stated, "Well, I've been married to a lot of women…they have all been named 'Jayne.'" They both laughed as Dad explained, "She's been skinny and not skinny; she's had short hair and long hair, blonde, brown, and frosted hair; she's worn glasses and contacts; she's been single and married; she's been a mom of one, two, three; a stay-at-home mom, a working mom; a room mother, a girl scout leader, a speech pathologist, a real estate agent, an antique enthusiast, a gardener; she's had different friends, sang in the church choir; and on and on. I've loved every version of her!"

Mom and Dad were married fifty-two years before mom passed three years ago. My buddy was at her life celebration and heard more versions of Mom and the reasons we loved her. Shortly thereafter, my buddy and his bride celebrated their twenty-fifth anniversary. My dad was pleased—he gives great advice.

As I looked at being with my love during the pandemic, I kept reflecting on this story and how the great love stories that surround my life have unfolded. When partners have the freedom and flexibility to express who they are in a relationship and the encouragement and acceptance to pursue ideas and dreams, love provides clarity. Be flexible.

Believe in the Supernatural

How do you get to Carnegie Hall? Practice, Practice, Practice. That's what I did. I had taken voice lessons since age ten and performed with the St. Louis Symphony Chorus for ten years. While with the chorus, I was honored twice to sing with a selected group of women at Carnegie Hall. It was during our second trip to sing Holst's "The Planets" onstage with the Harlem Boys Choir and the St. Louis Symphony Orchestra under the direction of its then-conductor, Leonard Slatkin. It was an out-of-this-world experience and one that is inexplicable, but I'll try my best.

The women of the chorus, including myself, stood on stage, in the middle, in a semicircle in front of the orchestra. The Harlem Boys Choir, dressed in trademark gray slacks, white shirts, ties, and maroon sweaters with traditional insignia, stood in front of us. As we started to sing with notes soaring higher and higher into the stratosphere, I focused on Conductor Slatkin's baton. It became mesmerizing as he swirled and pointed, creating the cues and tempo. I fixated my eyes on the movement of the wand; my ears, tuned to the rich blend of melodic harmony and dissonance; my breath expanded with every inhalation as it filled my chest and lungs.

With my eyes focused, Slatkin's baton turned blue. A bright electric blue, an ethereal glow, like a Stars Wars light saber, throwing off light, refracting from wall to wall, ten-feet, then twenty-feet, then thirty-feet. Blue light careened through the entire auditorium. I was flooded with a sense of peace and tranquility. I couldn't believe my eyes. But I knew I was not hallucinating when, while we were singing, a Harlem Choir boy turned around and looked up at me.

With tears streaming down his face, he whispered, "Do you see it? Can you see what's happening?"

I responded. "Yes."

I turned him around and we both kept singing until the performance ended in a standing ovation. As we hustled off stage, this little boy, whom I had never seen before this moment on stage, found me in the crowd. He hugged me tight.

"Were we the only ones who saw it?" he asked. "The whole hall went blue, right? It was so amazing! Why didn't everyone see it?"

I explained, "Sometimes God gives us a glimpse of Heaven but not all experience it at the same time."

I don't know that what I saw was truly a glimpse of Heaven, but it was unlike anything I'd ever seen or experienced before—or since. I don't know if others saw the phenomena that the Harlem Choir boy and I did; but to me, it explains how, in the same moment, two people can be seeing and hearing the same thing, but interpret and understand it differently.

To cut to the clarity, sometimes you have to believe that a situation, problem, opportunity, or possibility can be reimagined. We can choose multiple ways at any given moment to proceed through life; we are limited only by the choices we make and our own understanding.

Since that experience, I flip things upside down and think about them differently than they might first appear. I often revisit my focus on the blue light that filled Carnegie Hall and remind myself that there are, at any given moment, alternative ways of doing and seeing things to create peace and tranquility in our lives.

When I recall the moment I first heard of the worldwide pandemic and remember the fear that set in, I also recognize how I handled my stress.

1. I allowed myself to be me, to say and feel the things I needed to, to thrive through the uncertainty of the future.
2. I became flexible, accepting my living conditions and realizing there are more ways than one to see and experience something—anything. I looked at the pandemic and saw more than just how to survive out of a weekender bag without underwear. I saw the positive possibilities within the changes that accompanied the pandemic's social distancing, mask-wearing, and lockdowns. I accepted the inherent uncontrollability of my life.

3. I believe in the supernatural, and signs of and from the supernatural. During the seventeen months quarantined away from my St. Louis home, I received three distinct supernatural signs.

First, on my mom's birthday, I was taking pictures of a sunset over Folly River in South Carolina. I was concentrating on the photo so intensely that my love had to tell me to look to the right. My sweetheart pointed, "It's your mom on her birthday!" A cloud shaped like a winged angel filled me with hope.

Next, on the day I was to serve as a virtual music leader for a Christian conference, I walked out to the porch and snapped a quick picture of the sunrise. The sun shone like a cross, as if God was giving me a signal of encouragement before the conference.

Finally, on New Year's morning 2021, I heard the sound of doves. I had never heard that sound before at my boyfriend's home. I took it as a sign of peace.

Did I assign the meaning of hope, encouragement, and peace to these experiences, or were these supernatural signs I received at the time I needed them the most? To me, yes, these were supernatural signs: a glimpse of Heaven. Indeed.

From insurance to music teacher to elementary principal, Diane Finnestead returned to insurance in 2014. Recognized as a leading producer in life and health insurance nationwide, Diane advocates health reform through National Association of Health Underwriters, serving on the St. Louis board, and the National Speaker's Bureau. She is a sought-after virtual and stage speaker for conferences, summits, podcasts, radio shows, and webinars on topics of health insurance, Medicare, entrepreneurship, and business.

Diane credits her ability to help thousands of Americans find the right insurance over the past twenty years to her background and career in education.

Diane holds a bachelor's degree in music from the University of North Texas, two master's degrees from Webster University: one in teaching and one as an education specialist. She completed post-graduate work at the University of Memphis and Northwestern University.

Diane is thrilled to be a contributor to this anthology.

Please contact Diane below to share your glimpses of Heaven.
314-302-5743
Diane Finnestead You Tube
agents@dianeinsurancestl.com
www.dianeinsurancestl.com
https://www.LinkedIn.com/in/diane-finnestead-mat-Ed-s-4187912a/
https://www.Facebook.com/dianeinsurancestl

Networking:
How to Set Yourself Apart

Gisele Marcus, MBA

I grew up being told, "Head down, blinders on," "Do a great job, you'll get great rewards." No one told me that networking was part of the unwritten responsibilities in the job description.

I was offered an expatriate, a/k/a "expat," assignment in Johannesburg, South Africa, in 2009. An expat assignment is taking on a project, a position, for the same company but outside of your home country. During my expat assignment, I learned the criticality of networking.

Some companies, when they send you on an expat assignment, will tell you your next two assignments. This allows you to know, definitively, what your future roles will be, including title, job description, and the current team. Well, at my company, when you go on an expat assignment, there is no plan for your next job in the company—you have no "next" job assigned. This means you, yourself, have to secure your next job within the organization before your expat assignment ends.

How would this be done while you are outside of your home country? I asked my human resources director exactly that, i.e., how to ensure I had a job when I returned. She encouraged me to talk to the vice president and general manager (VP/GM) Global Energy & Workplace Solutions, a direct report to the president of my business unit, who signed off on all of the expat assignments in that unit. Surely, he would know the secret sauce to securing my next assignment as he had seen so many others do so prior to my inquiring.

To not appear overly concerned—though I really was—when I spoke to the VP/GM, I fashioned my conversation more like a story. I told him that

I had heard that a colleague, we'll call "Jim," had gone on an expat assignment in Europe, and when he returned three years later, he didn't have a job. His leadership team had changed (leaders he knew had left the company or gone to other areas of the business) and no one realized he had been missing for three years. This was unimaginable to me that an employee, who was out of sight, was really out of mind.

After listening to my concerns, the VP/GM responded, "Come back to the office once a quarter, meet with your sponsors, of which I will be one, and any and all of your mentors. Remind us that you are on an expat assignment, estimate when you will be coming home. Ideally, we would like to know six months in advance of your return. Why? As jobs are on the drawing board, we can consider you."

This was like a key to the palace! Not only did I receive direct advice to address my concern, but I acquired a sponsor, an executive-level leader, who was willing to support my elevation in the organization in the rooms where job placement determinations were made about high-level assignments. This VP/GM had a reputation of being brilliant and was very well respected throughout the organization and within the industry. Having him as a sponsor would enable my career trajectory to reach heights that were unimaginable without his support.

When Jim went to Europe, he was forgotten because he had not touched base with leadership to assist him in finding a new role. He had not networked. So I followed the instructions of my sponsor. I came home every quarter. I went to my office, met with each of my sponsors and mentors, and told them six months in advance when I would return. It worked in my favor.

What did I learn? Unlike what I was taught growing up, I learned that networking is important and part of the unwritten responsibilities in a job description.

What Networking Is...

1. Networking is connecting in an authentic, genuine way with another person. Not in a superficial way. Meaning you contribute to others without seeking anything in return. You offer assistance, share knowledge, or make valuable introductions.

2. Networking is developing a two-way relationship where each person derives benefit. Meaning, when I'm building a relation ship, I cannot be on the "Gisele" channel talking about myself all the time or constantly looking to derive something out of the relationship without depositing anything into the relationship.

When I was seeking a new job while on expat assignment, before meeting with each mentor and sponsor, I studied them—I read their bios; I went online, i.e., LinkedIn, Facebook, Twitter. If I knew someone who knew them, I'd ask about their favorite things. I created a cheat sheet with key information about them. At each meeting with my mentors and sponsors, I'd reference something I knew about them. For example, I knew South Africa was my VP/GM's favorite place on the planet to visit. So based on his being a tri-athlete (bike, run, swim competitor), at each quarterly meeting, I'd bring him something that was South-African branded, such as a t-shirt, glasses, hat, water bottle, and I'd inquire about his next competition.

What Networking Is Not...

1. Networking is not collecting business cards that you never follow up on and that eventually collect dust.
2. Networking is not talking to as many people as you can at a cocktail party.
3. Networking is not asking someone you don't know personally to do a favor (like find you your next job opportunity or get your child into an esteemed educational enrichment program).

How do you get or stay systematically connected?

1. At networking events, such as receptions, have opener/teaser questions ready to approach that other person in the room who doesn't appear to be speaking with anyone:

    a. What brought you here tonight?

    b. Are you a supporter of XYZ cause?

    c. Are you a native to (city of the event)?

    These openers create a great approach for someone who would rather not network because it allows the networker to connect with someone like themselves who is also likely uncomfortable in this space by the nature of their not speaking with anyone else at that moment.

2. Set a schedule. Connect with a person quarterly or every other month. Be intentional and systematic.

3. Document a plan. Who do you want to network with and how often? Here are actions you can take to connect:

    a. On their half yearly birthday, send them a birthday card. That will be unique. Who does that?

    b. Send articles on their favorite topics. This will gain the attention of your reader as it is specific to something they enjoy, admire, and/or have an interest in. One of my colleagues in St. Louis is a Washington University graduate. When I see a hard or soft copy of an interesting article about her school, I pop it in the mail with a nice note. "Mary-Thinking about you. Let's grab coffee." How do I do this? Google search allows you to create a query on topics of interest. Set it up. As you obtain articles on that topic, send to the person.

    c. Connect with others via social media of their choice using professional content. Selecting a medium of their choice (not your choice) will enhance the possibility of your content being seen by the person with whom you'd like to network.

    d. Send a handwritten or electronic note each season of the year. This is a differentiator. It's rare nowadays to receive a hand written note. Given our electronic world, this can also be scanned and emailed. As there is a trend for people working virtually, a handwritten message may not be viewed right away.

Remember, people have varying personality types.

There are extroverts, introverts, and ambiverts (a person who has a balance of both). Therefore, your networking prospect's personality type may differ from yours. Given this is a new relationship, you will not know at first. However, keep this in mind as you define your networking approach. You want to be cautionary in that you do not create a networking discomfort for the person with whom you are newly networking.

Using some of these strategies set me apart from the rest and assisted me while on my expat assignment in landing eleven internal job offers! So it works if you work it! I asked my VP/GM to help me think through my top three offers that were all based on my criteria for my next role: exposure to other executives, ability to attain my next desired position (yes, thinking two moves ahead), and ability to make an indelible imprint and be even more of a difference-maker in our organization. I selected an opportunity that led me on a path of my ultimate career goal: to run an international business just shy of one billion dollars in revenue, where I had responsibility for 1,200 employees across forty countries on five continents. This was unlikely if I had not networked.

Each networking story is different. What will be yours?

Gisele Marcus is a networking Expert, TEDx speaker, Harvard MBA, and first-generation college graduate. Raised in Harlem (neighborhood in upper Manhattan, New York City) when the neighborhood was plagued by blight, Marcus succeeded and soared in networking and public speaking above perceived limits and all odds against her.

Marcus's expertise lies in offering practical, implementable solutions and focuses her endeavors on networking, leadership, diversity, equity, and inclusion. She has been featured in the *Huffington Post*, *Black Enterprise* magazine, the *Milwaukee Business Journal*, the *St. Louis Business Journal*, and *Good Morning St. Louis*, a business talk show on the Fox-affiliate network. Marcus is known to deliver knowledge, inspiration, and customization to her talks, while sharing essential insights on industry trends with her audiences and clients.

Marcus serves as Professor of Practice in Diversity, Equity & Inclusion at the Olin Business School at Washington University in St. Louis, Missouri.

http://www.giselemarcus.com/
http://www.linkedin.com/in/giselemarcus/
gisele@giselemarcus.com
312-833-2633

Your Inner Success Formula

Rebecca Hall Gruyter

When you want success in your business or with your personal life goals, you likely have a checklist of "to-dos for success" that includes essential things like goal-setting, business plan, financial projections, marketing and sales strategies, hiring, and building relationships.

It's wonderful and exciting to check off those items, to see what you are bringing forth, to see the gains and results you've worked so hard to achieve! Things begin to fall into place and move forward; you're really on a path to success. Your heart is full and you're making a difference in the world!

Before too long, however, you begin to feel pressure, discomfort, anxiety, and even fear. These are emotions that are natural when we enter a new phase of growth. Things start to feel chaotic, out of our control, and overwhelming. We begin to wonder: *Is this success? Is this what I've worked so hard for?* This is what happened to me when I experienced my first rapid-growth business period.

I had overcome so many personal obstacles to take my first steps onto the path of truly sharing myself and my gifts with the world that I had a sense—an expectation, really—that once I "succeeded" it would be clear sailing.

What I discovered is that I needed more than a checklist. I needed to understand how ***Time, energy, and resources worked and flowed for me. These three elements must work together to create true success.*** For me, "true success" is when we not only achieve our business or personal goals, but we also are living a *life of purpose on purpose*, every day. I also discovered my ***Inner Success Formula.*** I became aware of how time, energy, and resources affect us: how time can work for or against us; how our particular energy can boost us or drain us; and how life isn't a solo journey—we have resources that can support us professionally and personally.

Everybody has the same twenty-four hours per day

The first element—time—is a good place to start because, once we address how we are using our time, our energy and resources will naturally follow! So let us begin shifting from chaos to clarity...

Why is it that when we achieve a level of success, we begin to feel that we're busier than ever, running around doing more and more things, feeling anxious, chaotic, and like we're constantly running out of time? How many times have you said, "I'm SO busy, I don't have enough time!" I call this the "full-plate syndrome." We already have so many things on our plates in life that success brings more opportunities and more responsibilities that fill our plates even more—to the point that they may overflow.

Imagine a beautiful buffet table before you and one dinner plate in your hands. Everything looks so delicious and tempting! You start to serve yourself, adding some of this and some of that to your plate. As it fills up, potatoes mix with vegetables, salad gets hidden, and the olives begin to roll off. You let the olives fall and try to fit a little bit more. Then you discover there's *another* table after this with more food, including your favorite desserts. But you don't have any more room on your plate, so you miss out on that chocolate cake!

Inner Success Tip: Stop the full-plate syndrome. Here is an exercise I use with my clients, which always helps them change their perspective as they evaluate what is on their plate. (Hint: Usually, we underestimate what is on our plate.)

Take a dinner-sized paper plate or draw a plate-sized circle on a piece of paper. Using sticky notes, write down all the things you do in a day, *one specific activity per note.* Stick each one on the plate. Great! Now, did you include taking a shower, brushing your teeth, getting dressed, combing your hair, preparing the meal, eating the meal, cleaning up after the meal, driving, and of course, sleeping?

The sticky notes are stacking up quickly, aren't they? Now go back through the notes and add how much *time each of those activities take.* Go ahead and try it. I believe you will soon realize that you are trying to fit many more hours into your day than twenty-four. Something has to change!

We choose how we can spend—and stretch—our time

When we are deep into "piling on our plates," we can forget that our activities come from the choices we're making. Yes, WE are in charge of choosing how we spend our time. The first time I was in growth mode, I regularly said to my husband, "I'm so busy...I have so much on my plate right now...I just can't take on that thing...I'm feeling so overwhelmed..."

At one point, he looked me dead in the eye, and said, "Well, *you* set your schedule...Isn't this *your* business?" He meant it kindly—and it was the exact wakeup call I needed! I began to look deeply. I questioned: *How am I spending my time? What am I building and what am I wasting? What do I REALLY want?*

I'm still learning how to work with full-plate syndrome (and my husband still lovingly reminds me when I'm getting off track). I believe this "syndrome" is a natural part of moving outside of our comfort zone to go for that next thing we are being called to bring forth. So it is important to learn how to recognize the full-plate syndrome and address it with tools that are right for us. Right for YOU.

What tools? There is no one perfect way, but I suggest creating your own checklist for your relationship with time. We are all wired differently, and our choices will vary according to where we are in our life's journey.

Inner Success Tip: Shift how you spend your time. Here is one way I shifted my relationship with time. My work with clients was getting more complex as they were growing in their own businesses. My conversations with them were, of course, also getting longer, but I hadn't recognized this. I just kept feeling like, *Why am I running behind schedule? Why is my day feeling so tight?*

I loved who I was working with, the conversations we had, and the deeper way I was serving my clients. Once I recognized how I was feeling and what was important to me, I chose a simple, yet powerful, solution: I reduced the number of appointments by five to ten a week and increased the length of times for each appointment I had (I also allowed more space between them for my self-care).

Yes, that's fewer clients I can talk to in a month, and it was difficult to do at first. But now I find that I can go deeper with them; I'm more present; our conversations are more effective and less of my time is needed later. I am able to serve more clients, save more time, and stay balanced.

What is one way you can shift how you spend your time so you feel more in balance and at choice?

How to discern what we want on our plate

After we look at how we are using time, we can decide with more clarity what we *do* want on our plate—what activities and opportunities are we choosing that are in alignment with our growth and purpose (personally, as well as professionally)?

To decide what you really want on your plate, I suggest creating some time to stop, step back, and answer the following questions: Which activities fill me up and which ones drain me? What am I saying *yes* to and why? What can I take off my full plate right now, **and what can I shift away from?**

Inner Success Tip: "Yes" is not always the answer. Moving forward doesn't always mean saying *yes* to every opportunity. Remember that each time you say yes to something you are adding it on to your plate. You have a choice at any time to say *no*—or even better, *not yet* or *not right now*.

It's important to consider the timing of things too. We can't do everything all at once. However, we can complete things, move them off our plate thus creating more room for new things as we move forward. So it is important to prioritize and know what is a yes now, a no now, and what is something to move forward at a later date. Maybe we need to grow further, have more systems in place, or make room on our plate for it to be time to say yes.

When we say yes to something, we might be saying no to something else that we don't know about yet which could be the perfect thing for us.

How do you know whether to say *yes, no,* or *not yet?*

With each opportunity that comes my way, I ask myself if it adds to *the way I am called to serve at the highest level*. My choices must align with who I am, who I want to be, or what I value. My Inner Success Formula requires exploration of the following questions:

▲ Whom do I want to serve now?

▲ How do I want to serve?

▲ How much do I want to serve?

▲ What are the best ways for me to deliver my gifts?

Inner Success Bonus Tip: Create some additional open space on your plate. By creating space, we are anticipating growth and making room for it in our life and business.

When we pay attention to our time, energy, and resources, and make choices based on the clarity of our observations, our choices help us change our behavior, which in turn supports doing those things that are in alignment with our unique blend of gifts, values, priorities, and life purpose. This, to me, is true success!

Rebecca Hall Gruyter is a global influencer, #1 international best-selling author and compiler, publisher, radio-show host (syndicated on fourteen different networks), and an empowerment leader who wants to help her clients and you, the reader, reach more people. Rebecca has built multiple media platforms and live events to help experts reach more people—including on radio and TV, in books and magazines, also creating the Speaker Talent Search—building a powerful promotional reach of over ten million!

Rebecca is the CEO of RHG Media Productions, which has helped 800-plus authors become best-sellers! She is the owner of Your Purpose-Driven Practice and creator of the Speaker Talent Search.

Hall Gruyter has personally contributed to thirty-plus published books and multiple magazines; she has been quoted in major media: *The Huffington Post*, ABC, CBS, NBC, Fox, and Thrive Global. She now helps experts to be quoted in major media too.

Rebecca wants clients to have impact! Be Seen, Heard and SHINE!

http://www.YourPurposeDrivenPractice.com
http://www.RHGTVNetwork.com
http://www.SpeakerTalentSearch.com
Rebecca@YourPurposeDrivenPractice.com
www.facebook.com/rhallgruyter
www.facebook.com/pages/Rebecca-Hall-Gruyter/442052769207010
www.linkedin.com/pub/rebecca-hall-gruyter/9/266/280
www.twitter.com/Rebeccahgruyter
Instagram: RHGTVNetwork
Pinterest: Rebecca Hall Gruyter

Conquering Compromised Decision-Making

Dr. Nadine L. Kouba

Have you ever come through a challenging and stressful situation and begun to question the decisions you made? You wonder whether you were thinking at all as you realize how poor those decisions were. Perhaps you discover that your choices were not only flawed but biased, too!

When faced with chaos, we all react. Whether it's freezing in disbelief, bucking ourselves up to fight the situation, or retreating to a safe place, our bodies often respond even faster than our minds can. In less than one second, we are ready to respond. Thousands of years of human survival have conditioned humans to react to chaos the same as we react to any threat. We fight, flee, or freeze. That stress reaction prepares our bodies to respond to the threat and affects how our brain and thought processes work.

I like to believe that *I'm* in control, not the situation. However, I recall attending a staff meeting shortly after I had successfully completed a highly visible project. As the project manager and lead contributor, I knew every step of the plan: the items completed, barriers overcome, the pilot results, in addition to the delivery plan and evaluations of the final product. If there was a question, I was the person called. The project was successful. And the company recognized my team's and my efforts.

So there I sat in our team meeting. Each team member provided an update on their current projects. One colleague's report indicated things were not going well. Our boss began to ask more in-depth questions about the "troubled" project. And tension started to grow in the room. Each of us recognized our colleague was struggling with the project. With each question, the rest of us became more uncomfortable, and our stress levels increased. No one wanted to be in the spotlight next.

Suddenly, my boss turned to me and asked about how I'd handled some similar detail on my recently completed project. Under his gaze and the stress level in the room, nothing came to mind. I could not recall any details about my project. I knew I'd done it, but no information surfaced. I stammered, "Let me check my notes and get back to you this afternoon." The meeting concluded, and we all got up to return to our desks. As we walked down the hall, all the information about my project came flooding back into my memory! At the same time, I realized that I was no longer feeling stressed.

So what happens to our thinking when we are highly stressed?

You may be familiar with what happens to the body when the fear reaction ("fight, flight, freeze response") kicks in. Cortisol, testosterone, and adrenaline are instantly released; and the sympathetic nervous system also reacts to prepare our muscles to flee or fight. Our blood pressure goes up. We breathe more rapidly and more substantial blood flow goes to our core. Other bodily processes shut down, including digestion and our immune system. The released cortisol slams the door closed between the limbic part of the brain and the upper part of the brain (the neocortex and prefrontal cortex) leaving us with only the emotional part of the brain to make our decisions. Without access to the neocortex (which holds the memory of how to do things) and the prefrontal cortex (which contains the "executive" brain where strategy, creativity, integrity, innovation, ethics, and trust reside), we humans can make only emotional decisions.

When the door closes between the limbic and executive brain, we make decisions using our limbic brain. It's all part of the survival process. Quick reactions are required to protect ourselves from threatening situations. There is no need for higher-order thinking. A deadline can cause the same response that facing a sabertoothed tiger or a gun would.

In my example, I became stressed by the situation in the meeting. The released cortisol promptly went to my brain and shut the doors to my neocortex. My limbic brain retained the memory of the project, but I could not access the memories contained in my neocortex for the details of how the project was completed. It was only after leaving the stressful meeting and walking (body movement) that the grip of cortisol was broken, and I was allowed to re-access my neocortex.

Humans were built to survive, and our brain function underscores that purpose. It's helpful to learn about some intense research focused on human brain function conducted over the last fifty years to combat compromised decision-making. Here are just a few findings that may help our understanding.

In 1951, Kurt Lewin found, "Behaviour is the function of the person and the environment." How we think and react is based on our reaction to the situation or environment we are in.

Daniel Kahneman, a Nobel prizewinner in economics, researched the brain and flaws in how we think. He concluded that there are two systems in the brain. System 1 is fast, instinctive, emotional. In other words, the stimulus comes in through the limbic brain first, and we have an emotional reaction. System 2 is the logical piece that occurs after we make an emotional decision. The question is: How soon after the emotional response and decision will System 2 commence? In my example, System 2 didn't kick in until I left the meeting and started walking down the hall.

Take a moment to think about a compromised decision you have made. Recall the decision, then determine how long it took you to realize it was compromised. How long did it take System 2 to start after your compromised decision? Minutes? Hours? Days? Or not yet?

The limbic brain is where our conscious and unconscious biases reside. Often when making a compromised decision, we include our biases, conscious and unconscious; and we aren't aware that we've made a biased decision. However, when we analyze a compromised decision later, we will often find bias is evident.

Another concern is that cortisol has a twenty-six-hour shelf life. It can compromise our decision-making for an entire day. And if we are triggered again during that day, the cortisol clock resets for an additional twenty-six hours, thus allowing our limbic brain to control our decision-making even longer. Some people struggle with breaking cortisol's grip because they are triggered daily.

How can we best combat compromised decision-making? Fortunately, there are more than a dozen ways. Here are just a few to break the hold of cortisol and regain access to your executive brain

1. Recognize that every reaction you have to a situation or your environment will be emotional to start. The limbic brain will process the information first in a fast, instinctive, and emotional way.

2. Breathe. Pausing to breathe allows you to stop your emotional response. Some people employ specific breathing techniques. One technique I find helpful is "square breathing." You inhale to the count of four, hold your breath for the count of four, exhale to the count of four, and pause to the count of four. Repeat the cycle eight to ten times. By concentrating on breathing and counting, you control your thoughts, which in turn calms the mind and allows you to apply logic to the situation.

3. Move. Take a twenty-minute walk or exercise for twenty minutes. Body movement helps to burn off the cortisol and allows your brain to access your executive brain.

4. Speak or meet with a trusted colleague, friend, or loved one. When we interact with people we trust and care about, it causes oxytocin, the bonding hormone, to flow and throw open the doors to our executive brain.

5. Laugh. When we laugh, oxytocin flows and opens the access to our executive brain. Even gallows humor can cause oxytocin to stream if you are with trusted colleagues or friends.

6. Meditation. The practice of meditation causes us to take control of our thoughts, focus, and relax. We can more clearly focus on decision-making after a refreshing meditation.

7. Prayer. Prayer helps us to focus our thoughts. Seeking support from a higher power lets us refocus our thinking.

8. Trust your training. In school and at work, we practice fire and tornado drills. When faced with one of those emergencies, we follow the routines we've practice and evacuate. If there are situations that trigger you, consider creating your practice drill. By clearly outlining how you will respond to a stress-producing situation, you prepare yourself to act in that way when the problem occurs. You can trust your training and react logically after experiencing the initial emotion.

We all react instinctually and emotionally immediately in a situation. Understanding why we respond to our environment the way we do, allows us to engage our logical decision-making abilities more quickly. And we reduce the compromised decisions we make and, just maybe, no longer question if we've done the right thing.

Nadine L. Kouba, Ph.D., is a trained and certified professional executive coach. She works with leaders to increase their effectiveness and accelerate their business growth and profitability. With over twenty-five years of experience working with individual contributors and leaders at all levels across the United States and globally in the Asia Pacific region, the Middle East, and Europe, she brings a unique perspective from working in seven different industries to her client engagements. In addition, she's coached clients in the federal government, educational institutions, and nonprofits.

Nadine owns and operates Kouba Coaching, LLC. Currently, she serves as the president of the ICF St. Louis Chapter. You can reach her by email at nadine@koubacoaching.com or calling her voice mail, 641-715-3900 Ext 968308#

Don't Put Me in A Box!

Jaime Zografos

"Open the door, Dad! Let me in!" my sister, Susan, would scream. "Let Jaime out of there!" Susan would scream and bang outside the bathroom or bedroom door, wherever and whenever Dad chose to trap me in. I was an eight-year-old girl locked in a room with my dad and nobody knows what happened to me in there.

My sister is one-and-a-half years older than me. She has always looked out for me since I can remember. She doesn't look after me like any regular sister, though; she looks after me in a special way that not many would understand. Nights that I was not locked in my dad's bedroom, I would sleep in my shared bedroom with Susan, who did goofy things that I never understood, until now.

Our twin beds were on wheels, and she would pull my bed over to hers, so the beds would touch. She would then lay her arm across my chest, and pretend to be asleep. It was annoying to me, and I would throw her arm off me over and over again, eventually making it a game. But it wasn't a game, I know, now that I am forty-five and understand what was happening. Susan was making sure nobody would take me from the bedroom; it was her way of keeping me safe!

In November 2020, I went to a week-long meditation retreat. The energy was powerful. Starting the first meditation of the first morning, I was "all in." I wanted to learn how to heal anything inside me. I didn't want anything else to be "wrong" with me! I was already divorced twice and a cancer survivor, all before the age of forty. I wanted to create love, abundance, and peace in my life.

To start that first meditation, I closed my eyes and followed the facilitator's guidance.

"Breathe."

I took a deep breath and saw a little girl curled up, as small as she could be, in a ball waiting for someone to save her from the bad things happening to her. She was alone in a dark space and I was looking over her. I reached down to her and held her. I raised her up in the light, to angels to take her out of the scary place of fear and pain.

When the meditation ended, tears were rolling down my face. *This is not how this was supposed to go,* I thought to myself. *This is supposed to be a happy time! I am at a retreat, creating love and peace, not crying over childhood memories.*

That was how the week began.

In that first meditation, I was my adult self facing the reality that something had happened to my younger self in that room, a reality I had buried for forty-four years. I saw that little girl; I saw the trauma; I wanted to save her. I was petrified to go into any more meditations because I did not want to know what else happened.

I continued the retreat and kept doing the meditations with the intention of not going back to "that" dark place, but to stay in the place of love and light. I followed all the rules of the retreat until the third day when I met some friends and we decided to grab food and drinks in the evening. This was not allowed in the rule book.

I have a very social side, so this was easy for me to turn to. It only takes a few drinks to have a few more and then one too many. But I was scared and this was the way I knew to avoid learning anything else about me. Remember, I did not want anything else to be "wrong" with me, because who would want me or love me then? I drank because of that scared little girl inside me being locked in a room with her dad and never learning how to healthfully "connect" with a man.

Let me circle back to my younger self for a moment. My mom and dad divorced when I was seven- or eight-ish; my mom remarried when I was nine. My sister and I would go to our dad's for visitation, and I would come back home with horrible stomachaches that would last for days. These stomachaches were pure agony and seemed to last forever.

I can't recall many moments at my dad's apartment, but I recall feelings in my body, not actual events. I have no recollection of his place except the stairwell to his front door, the small kitchen table, and the room where we played Atari. The other memories are gone or buried.

Susan and I have had long talks about what happened at Dad's apartment. She has explained to me that one night out of every weekend at Dad's place I had to sleep in his bedroom with the door locked. He would not let me out, nor her in. Susan told me she would bang on the door and scream, but couldn't get to me; Dad would yell at her to stop. Imagine how alone, scared, and confused Susan felt. When we went back home, Susan would tell Mom what happened. I never had anything to say except that my stomach hurt.

In January 1989, I was twelve years old and was in a courtroom to change my last name as my dad gave up legal rights to us. We were adopted by our stepdad. Why didn't my real dad want us anymore? Was this to close the chapter on my *old* childhood and start new? I thought this was going to be wonderful, and maybe it was for a few years; but my mother and step-father divorced in 1992.

Childhood trauma follows a person. I am a forty-five-year-old single woman now and none of my intimate relationships have worked out for me. I have married twice and have dated for six years, since my second divorce in 2015. I have had more "brief" relationships than anyone I know, very few going past five or six weeks—and I would be the "runner" most often, but not always. This has come to be an embarrassing and shameful part of me.

In 2020-2021, it started getting worse. I started seeing a new counselor three months ago for other reasons, but my "patterns" are now the main topic. It took me years of dating, and the help of my counselor, to even notice my patterns. I learned that one of my patterns was not knowing how to connect on dates; therefore, I drank. Another pattern was running. Anytime I felt "boxed" in, my fight or flight response activated. My response **was always flight. I RAN!** I ran from anything that felt good; and went to the next person. I learned distrust was a pattern; I learned I feared someone else trying to control me—much like Dad locking me in a room. I feared losing all control and just went to the next person.

In socializing, cocktails are the norm; this was never an issue for me—until it was. Until I chose to look at it. After looking back at multiple situations where I could not recall the events of the prior evening, I learned I was not putting myself into good situations. I was not making decisions that were authentic to me because I was drinking too much, creating connections out of numbness, which was the only way I knew.

So now what??? What we resist, persists, right?

My clarity through chaos!

I am the common denominator in my life. I am the only one that can change it. I am the only one that can face the reality that something happened to me in the bathroom/bedroom at my dad's house. If I want to have a healthy intimate relationship, I need to accept the trauma. I do not need to relive it; I do not need to own it as my fault. I do need to understand how is affects me with the patterns and decisions I create going forward.

I stopped drinking alcohol on September 18, 2021, to be able to gain clarity in my life. I have come across people, places, and things since that moment that have opened the door to accepting the trauma. I am done masking what happened to me. Nobody can save Jaime, but Jaime. I am not the little girl crawled up in a ball anymore. I get to honor, love, and respect myself. I get to make decisions I am proud of. I get to put myself in situations that are good for me. Most importantly, nothing is "wrong" with me. I was trapped in a room by my father as a young girl, and I couldn't get out! The chaos has played out in my life long enough and now, with clarity, I am **FREE.**

AND I have the world's greatest sister ever!

Jaime Zografos is an entrepreneur, mother of two beautiful young women, #1 international best-selling author, and soon to be podcast host. Jaime is the CEO of Jaime Z Enterprises, a diversified business portfolio engaged in real estate valuation, health and wellness, and the subscription-box industry.

Jaime's entrepreneurial spirit began over twenty years ago when she founded JZ Appraisals, specializing in residential appraisals across the St. Louis area.

In 2018, Jaime leveraged her business acumen with the opening of two OsteoStrong franchises, which provides increased strength and better balance, with a focus on bone density; ultimately improving members' quality of life.

Recently founded and still in its infancy, Crateful is the business behind Jaime's life mission. Crateful is a luxury personal development subscription box model creating personalized packages for our members. Crateful focuses on inspiration and empowering women to magnetize what they want in their life.

www.jaimezenterprises.com
hello@abundancedelivered.com
www.linkedin.com/in/jaime-zografos-8693a9a6
www.facebook.com/jaime.ladendorf/
www.instagram.com/jaime.zeee/

Pick Me

Sydney Zografos

I am a first born. I love order, patterns, schedules, routine, certainty…you get the picture. I spent a portion of my life being an only child, so I like attention too. With this in mind, being prioritized by others has always been important to me. I'm not sure if this is a product of being first-born, but I find it hard to adapt to a situation in which I am not the first thought.

Growing up, I felt I was never a priority. My sister and I are four and a half years apart, so I had a decent portion of time in which it was me, my parents, and I. However, my parents divorced when I was nine years old. I'd like to sit here and say it was rough, sad, and unexpected, but I saw it coming.

My mom sat me down and told me she and my dad were divorcing. Since I expected this, it was not a large event in my life. My sister, being the four-and-a-half-year-old she was, was unaware of the definition of "divorce." She was fine with the news because she wouldn't remember life any other way. Apparently, however, my once-four-year-old sister received the brunt of the divorce, according to my parents and everyone. I felt as if it should have been me: I should have been felt sorry for, doted upon…but I wasn't. I felt like I had to offer a sense of security and stability to my little sister; when in reality, I was the one who needed it.

Again, the divorce was not a large event in my life. I wouldn't mark it as some turning point where I realized things, saw the world differently, et cetera. It was more the events that followed that was the large event. Being my first-born self, I had a very hard time going from house to house with no real schedule. I needed order. I needed stability.

After the divorce, my dad changed. He wasn't so much a dad anymore but a babysitter. Going to his house was a vacation. We never ate meals of any nutritional value; but Thursday nights, we always went out for Mexican! He bought the snacks I wasn't allowed to have. My mother would have died if she had realized what we were eating at my dad's house. He took us late to soccer practices and school. My sister and I couldn't stand the scent of his laundry detergent, so he never washed our clothes. He promised to come to my softball games, but always worked late on Tuesdays. I'll spare you the rest of the details; let's just note that he missed my softball games. The divorce meant that my dad had to figure out a new balance and order, not only for himself but for my sister and I too. And he's never been one for balance or order. My order-craving self struggled with my dad because I needed something that he had no idea how to provide.

During that time, my mother was dating one of my favorite humans: my soccer coach. This guy was one of the coolest people I had ever met. He had been my soccer coach for quite a few years. My mother never told me when they were dating. I was nine years old, my parents had just gotten divorced, so I understand why she didn't come right out and say it. I don't remember the exact moment in which it occurred to me that my mother was dating my coach, but I figured it out. I was unsure how to feel with this knowledge. Did my teammates know? How do I explain that I'm now carpooling with my coach to practice? These were all questions racing through my nine-year-old mind. But what wasn't racing through my mind was if what I was eating had any nutritional value, if I was going to get to practice on time, or if he was going to be at my games.

His "like-ness," however, faded. My mom and he were great in the beginning. I loved that he made me a priority; it was something my dad didn't do. Like I said though, it faded: he and my mom fought. They fought like no other. Ever since I'd known him, he had chosen his words quite articulately. Even in their arguments, he spoke poetically, almost to point of fault. I never understood why my mother fought with him so harshly; he was awesome.

During their fights, it was my responsibility to fend for everyone else—I'm the oldest, right? Mom and my coach fought for hours. At the beginning they fought in front of my sister and me. Then they started shielding it from us. This didn't make it better—in fact, this was worse. It was my responsibility to tell my little sister that they were upstairs or in their room, because I couldn't break it to them that they were fighting—again. I was no one's priority at this time. My soccer coach, whom I loved and admired, was always fighting with my mom. All of his time when he was occupied with fighting with my mother, I only saw the not-so-great and the coaching parts of him.

To this day, I find myself craving security and stability in my life. My present relationships sometimes struggle if I am not a person's first thought. This is ironic, though, because I lived with not being prioritized for so long. I thought I was fine.

It wasn't until I came to college I realized all that I was missing. To paint the picture: I am a black-haired, twenty-two-year-old girl, studying English and psychology in the Midwest. The second I got a glimpse of someone *wanting* me, *needing* me, *prioritizing* me, I could never look back. I met a person that did this for me, day in and day out, no questions asked. My friend made me feel loved and appreciated for the person I was, admiring how "strong" I was. Really, though, I was looking for someone to be the strong one. It was a role I had played for much too long, and I was ready to pass the baton. I found that in my best friend. They made me work for it though, don't get me wrong. I met them at a time when I was looking to care for someone, and they were looking to be cared for. I think that's why we were such a good match from the onset; we had an immediate connection, and I could never quite place my finger on why. At that point in my life, I felt like I always had to "work" to be made a priority. My friend made me feel like I was the coolest black-haired, twenty-two-year-old girl, studying English and psychology in the Midwest there ever was. That is, until they didn't.

I think that was my pivotal moment. They gave me what I needed when I needed it most, but that was all I got. Moving down their priority list was the hardest move I've ever made. It's what I needed, though, and they knew it.

After the move down their priority list, I realized I was okay. I realized I was equipped to prioritize myself, rather than depending on someone else to do it for me. I guess that's what I learned…that was my clarity. If I want to be prioritized by other people, I need to prioritize myself. I think this goes with anything. Ever heard the phrase, "You have to love yourself before someone else can love you"? Same rule applies to prioritizing yourself. I am still working on this, of course, and honestly, I'm not great at it. I still lean on my friend tremendously, but they don't give in. I think I will remain stagnant on their priority list, but it is because they care about me and want to see me make *me* the top of my own priority list. Does that make sense? They care about me and I need to know that.

Being alone used to be something I was terrified of, but not anymore. I never used to cook before, but I cook now. I cook for myself, sometimes for my roommates, but mostly for myself. I go to yoga. I used to not be able to do that alone, but now I'm great at it; in fact, I sometimes prefer to go alone. I watch television alone and enjoy it. All wins to my priority list.

The point is, there are people in this world who will not make you feel like a first priority in their lives; and there are people who will make you feel like you are that cool, black-haired, twenty-two-year-old girl, studying English and psychology in the Midwest and that you are their top priority. These people may stay, or leave, but *you* will always be there for yourself.

Moving up your own priority list is a momentous task, but one that *can* be accomplished.

Sydney found her love for writing recently, as she was reluctantly convinced by her roommate that she should pursue a career in such.

When she is not writing, Sydney loves capturing candid photos with disposable cameras, listening to any sort of music she can get her hands on, and spending time with friends.

Sydney is currently finishing her career at Rockhurst University with a BA in English and psychology and a minor in general business. She plans on purchasing a one-way ticket to Europe after graduation, with hopes of one day starting her own record company with her best friend.

sydneynzografos@gmail.com
https://www.instagram.com/sydzog/
https://www.linkedin.com/in/sydney-zografos-836411196/

The Emotional Roller Coaster

Karen L. Fox

The year was 2010. I couldn't contain my joy! I was giddy, sitting on a plane with several friends headed to San Francisco—one of my favorite places in the world. I felt like a kid in a candy store. We were headed to Marcia Weider's Dream Coach Conference, "Inspiring Speakers." I had dreamed of attending this event for over twenty years.

I first heard Marcia at a business conference. She was on stage speaking to thousands and asked, "If you could do anything in the world and knew you couldn't fail, what would that be?" It was like she was speaking directly to me. My heart beat faster and a resounding *yes* went off in my mind. I knew exactly what I would do: become a SPEAKER!

Let's take a step back to 1982 when this story really began. Mike and I had been married a couple of years when we agreed I should start my "fun" job with Home Interiors, a home décor direct sales company, while working full-time at a florist in St. Louis, Nettie's Flower Garden. I had wanted to join Home Interiors since I was sixteen; however, by law I had to be eighteen. So, I waited.

Once I was working in home décor, I loved helping people decorate while I built relationships with hostesses and customers. I was great at both and recognized as top in sales my first year in the business. It wasn't long before this fun part-time job became my fun full-time job. I couldn't imagine doing anything else. I was one of the youngest in the company promoted to manager, which was no easy feat. As a manager, I had the privilege of training and supporting women as they worked toward their success, while continuing to build amazing leaders and teams. Watching others' success fueled my fire to want to do more. Talk about an adrenaline rush. Happy endorphins at a high daily dose coursed through my body!

Zig Ziglar used to say, "You can have everything in life you want, if you will just help other people get what they want." This concept came naturally for me and made it easy to get up every morning for my job and work late every night. I have heard the saying, "If you find something you love so much you would do it for free, you will never work a day in your life." That was my life. It wasn't work. It was joy. My life was amazing. I ate, drank, and slept Home Interiors and all the wonderful experiences and people that came with it.

I continued to grow and move up the career path with promotion after promotion. Life was grand. I was recognized in the top three percent of the company in sales and recruiting. I won trips, awards, and bonuses for not only my personal sales and recruiting but also for my teams' and managers'. I was among a select group as our team generated almost two million dollars in sales for the year. Keep in mind, this was all before internet sales.

Oh, the adrenaline flow is invigorating when crossing the stage to get your sales and recruiting awards; the immense pride is something completely different, though, when you are crossing the stage to get your fifteen- and twenty-year awards. The last proud milestone for me was walking across the stage with my husband, Mike, and daughter to accept my twenty-five-year diamond bracelet. My career had created a lifestyle for all three of us.

Anyone remember 2008 with the economic downturn and bailouts? December 2008 was when my life changed dramatically. It started out as an ordinary day, sun shining, but cold, as I was driving to meet my husband. I received a phone call from my husband's phone number, but the person on the other end was not my husband. He said, "Your husband has been in an accident."

My heart sank. I barely heard the gentleman say my husband was okay because my mind instantly transported me back to 2003 when we were hit head-on.

"Okay" wasn't exactly accurate though. Mike had flipped three times and had to be cut out of his vehicle. The only thing that stopped him from landing in a cold, icy lake was a single row of barbed-wire fence. We were extremely grateful. The driver had fallen asleep, crossed the highway, and t-boned him. We were also thankful for Mike's fast thinking and his angels. The fire chief said that if Mike had turned the other direction to avoid the accident, it would have taken his life, as well as the two occupants in the other vehicle.

After the 2008 accident, my husband's company merged two locations and moved out of state. We had a decision to make. We had both lived in the St. Louis area our entire lives and all our family was here. We opted to stay where we were and for Mike to look for another job.

Then the next blow came. The unthinkable happened. My heart was broken—no, thank God, it had nothing to do with our daughter. Everything I had been attached to for the past twenty-seven years stopped. In that second. I could hardly breathe. My world changed overnight. The fifty-year-old company I worked for and adored had closed their doors. How could this be happening?

Remember the Inspiring Speakers conference in San Francisco? Picture this: Two years after the company closed, I was sitting in the front row of that world-renowned conference, which I had anticipated attending for twenty years, right next to my best friend Cathy and other amazing friends. I was on top of the world. I had started a marketing company, "Karen THE Connector LLC." I had amazing clients, support of my husband, daughter, mom, and friends, when all of a sudden, the depths of despair and overwhelming oppression of my company's closure two years earlier hit me again. The downhill emotional roller coaster engulfed me right there in the front row. In my mind I cried, *NO! This can't be happening again, especially not now in the front row at the event I had waited twenty years to attend*! I thought I had gotten past the ups and downs. I should be over this. Yet, this time was different.

I heard the words clearly, "You lost your identity." This was my answer from God. It was the answer to the real problem. You see, everything I was and everything I did in life was wrapped up in my job. Everyone knew me by my company, knew me by my training workshops and humorous skits. I was used to walking into a room and everyone motioning me over to sit with them because they wanted to pick my brain. I was a leader, full of creativity, energy, and positivity.

I had led by example and was used to being at the top of my company. After my company of twenty-seven years had closed, however, I wanted to be invisible. I felt like I was a nobody without the visibility of the company. I wore dark clothing instead of my favorite color, red. This previous social butterfly didn't talk to people and dreaded going to events. I sat in the back, quietly, when I had been the one who always got to events early to get a front-row seat like I did on that day at the conference.

This was not me. But really, the only thing that had happened: I lost my identity.

I would love to tell you, after receiving my Divine revelation that day at the conference, that the angels came out singing *Hallelujah* and everything changed in that magical moment. It didn't. Just like grief, it takes time. But understanding the "why" allowed me to heal.

I had to come to the hard realization that doors in life close, while others open. I had to learn I had nothing to do with the events of my company's closure. I could not have controlled the outcome of my company—or everyone knows, I would have. It didn't change who this wonderful, caring, dynamic person was inside; it only changed how I viewed myself. My mind held me captive.

Learning I had attached my identity to my job changed everything. I can't say it made it easy or that it happened overnight, but knowing it allowed me to open my mind to embrace my future.

May I encourage you, if you have experienced the loss of a loved one or a job; if your children have gone to college or you have retired or experienced a divorce; if you've had a serious accident or something life-threatening; if you are a survivor or have made a major move—or anything else—please do not let your mind convince you that you are connected to those events. Please do not lose your identity like I did. The world needs you! Embrace your wonderful, loving, kind self, and continue to be a gift to the world.

Passionate about helping build leaders and their teams, Karen Fox is a business development coach, trainer, strategist, and speaker.

As an industry leader, she sees and holds a greater vision of success for her clients long before they do. She inspires and motivates them to experience extraordinary success.

Karen is excited to share her Extraordinary Success System with business owners and leaders who work with virtual teams, especially now when virtual team members feel lonely, isolated, and unengaged due to the 2020 pandemic. The three pillars she builds on are leadership, communication, and collaboration.

She is known for her humor in building successful and engaging teams. Some of her secret ingredients include creativity and experiential learning while honing the skills and sales personalities of leaders and teams. Her system creates greater productivity, retention, and engagement.

Karen is a John Maxwell speaker and trainer, Market Domination Strategist, and Master NLP Practitioner.

More information about Karen's work can be found at:
KarenTHEConnector.com
Karen@KarenTHEConnector.com
http://facebook.com/KarenTHEConnector
http://linkedin.com/in/KarenLFox
http://twitter.com/SocialKaren
http://instagram.com/KarenTHEConnector

Is Clarity Worth the Aggravation?

Joanne Weiland

On 11 September 1940, Prime Minister Winston Churchill spoke to his nation, addressing the situation Britain was then facing. They were in the middle of a chaotic war and being bombed. Citizens and soldiers hunkered in trenches where they hoped to stay out of harm's way. Churchill's advice to his people, "Stay calm, carry on."

Decades later, a drama queen emerged. Do you know any drama queens? They are everywhere.

I used to be quite the drama queen. I'd listen to a friend's narrative about how bad things had gone in their life and would pay enough attention to figure out what was going on, then I would jump in and tell them how bad my life was. If they had a mean step-parent, I had two mean step-parents. If they had events in their past that lead to their misfortunes, I had sadder, more depressing, tragic events in my past to draw everyone's attention and make them feel sorry for me. Then one day I decided my poor-me attitude was getting me nowhere. I had to tell a new story.

I'll always be thankful to Norman Vincent Peale, who I found when I was in my twenties, and through whose writings I learned the power of positive thinking. For years, I listened to Peale's tapes in my car; I read and reread his books. But his messages took years to penetrate my one-track mind. I stayed stuck in my trenches, many of which were deep ruts, like when your car gets stuck in the snow and you try to get out but dig a deeper and deeper trench by spinning your wheels. You need a bucketful of ashes for traction or you will continue to be stuck.

In terms of our thoughts, we will continue to think like we've always thought, behave like we've always behaved, until we create new tracks filled with different thoughts, positive thoughts—our mind's bucketful of ashes, so to speak, our traction.

Silly, but just when I would think I was making progress in changing my thoughts, the phone would ring or I'd have a talk with a family member or friend and would go back to my old game of one-upmanship. Back then, women shared stories about the births of their children. If a friend told me of her hard labor for six hours, I told her of my harder labor for seven hours, that I had to have an emergency C-section, that doctors said, if I didn't sign the surgery consent forms immediately, that my baby and I would die.

Slowly, Peale's words sunk in. I learned to listen and not respond with a dramatic story of my own. I continued reading and listening to Peale and other uplifting authors who became like new friends, the type of friends who would help me rise rather than fall.

I started going to church with my young son and to hang out with more positive people. Most were delightful; however, many told what they referred to as their "testimony," which I found to be similar to their old stories with a different label. They would talk about their lives and how bad they were until they were saved, all while seeming miserable. Sounded to me like recalling/retelling their stories kept them locked in the past and squarely out of the present.

It amazes me how many people would tell me their entire life stories, either on a plane or in line at the supermarket, without knowing my name or anything about me. Maybe it's my smile that made them feel comfortable with me; but it's as if they had a broken record playing in their heads and it's all they could think about.

When I decided to listen to my own broken records, if I didn't like what I was hearing, I commanded that story to leave. But the story fed off my anger and continued to play no matter how many times I commanded it to stop. At church, they told us to say things like "Get thy behind me, Satan!" But that didn't work either. Finally, my search for answers taught me to listen to the voice within me without anger. By releasing the anger, I could question my story and separate truth from drama. Gradually, my old stories stopped repeating themselves as I filled myself with new uplifting stories.

I couldn't destroy the negative stories totally, but I could transform them into positive stories.

Today, I recognize how I came to be the person I am. I am grateful. And when I am grateful for who I have become, my attitude and demeanor change and my light becomes brighter. I've learned that "fake it till you make it" is real. You may not feel like being happy, but if you pretend to be happy, you will become happy. *Whatever the mind of a man (or a woman) can conceive and believe, it can achieve.* Your feelings become thoughts; your thoughts become words; your words become action; your actions become character. So always be aware of your feelings and thoughts.

Today, I surround myself with positive people. I believe it is okay to get down, but I choose not to stay down in the negative trenches. We're here to support one another, not to compete and determine who has the worst husband, parents, children, upbringing, and so on.

I found the average person stays in chaos because they're scared to change their situation. They would prefer to do something else, such as start a business, return to school, et cetera; however, it's easier for them to stick to their old habits than to venture out and try something new.

I believe the world would be a lot happier place if everyone did what they loved and loved what they did. Sounds so simple. But how many people do you know who aren't doing what they love and loving what they do? We must step outside our comfort zone. We must find clarity and understand who we are.

What is your life purpose? What are you willing to do to achieve your goals?

When I discovered people who were doing what they loved twenty years ago, it was refreshing. Many of them had been downsized from corporate America and became entrepreneurs. Now, they have thriving businesses and are able to teach others how to become entrepreneurs, business owners; they have expanded and elevated current businesses or forged new career paths, among other things. And if they do the work, they can accomplish their dreams and goals with ease.

For me, when I was downsized, I took personality tests and found I was a connector. I thought, *How silly. Everybody is a connector.* Then

I tried to remember the last time someone connected me to someone else. I decided to figure out how to make a living as a connector. It took ten years but it was worth it. During that time, I was a mentor for MBA students at the University of Tampa and was blessed to work with students from all over the world. These students helped me develop systems, processes, and procedures that simplified connecting people with the experts they needed in order to advance in their lives.

In 2007, I obtained a blueprint to create a new way to implement ideas. Through that blueprint, I began connecting clients with experts. Clients were able to review the experts' credentials, engage in a seven-minute strategy session with the expert, and hire them in minutes. Together, the client and the expert then implemented ideas fast and easily. Because the expert has the connections the client needs and the education, experience, and expertise to put ideas into action and finish the project, the client's life can be transformed.

We all come into this world with a mission, a purpose, a calling. And when we're on track, our lives are calm and joyful because we're doing what we were designed to do. That doesn't mean everything goes smoothly. We often need help with our mission and vision. And as we complete parts of our life's purpose, we expand and we receive new desires and new ideas. We can live in bliss because, when we do what we love and love what we do, life is magical. Be grateful for everything in your life, and you'll see that all things work out for your benefit.

On 11 September 1940, Prime Minister Winston Churchill said, "Stay calm, carry on." This wisdom translates to the chaotic war within our own thoughts, thoughts that keep us stuck in patterns and lifestyles: My advice, "Get out of the trenches, get clarity, stay calm, and carry on."

So, my final question to you is: Is clarity worth the aggravation? I think so.

▲ ▲ ▲ ▲ ▲

Postscript: For years, the below quote by Simone Weil irritated me, but now I am beginning to understand its depth:

In what concerns divine things, belief is not appropriate. Only certainty will do. Anything less than certainty is unworthy of God.

Joanne Weiland invents industries. She is the founder of LinktoEXPERT Collaboration Cloud Community, which connects executives, entrepreneurs, event professionals, and the media worldwide. LinktoEXPERT assists clients in taking their businesses online, securing more speaking engagements, and creating more streams of income. Through Collaboration Cloud Community, clients can find an expert, review their credentials, and hire them in minutes. Members of this online community create their messages; and LinktoEXPERT, with its unique database exchange program, distributes them to decision-makers all over the world.

Joanne persistently networks, building relationships and joint ventures. She is continually interviewed on podcasts and radio shows worldwide and was a "growth hacker" before she knew that measuring marketing results was growth hacking.

Joanne encourages everyone to be all they are designed to be. Be seen. Be heard. Be known worldwide with ease!

jweiland@LinktoEXPERT.com
https://www.LinktoEXPERT.com
https://www.JoanneWeiland.LinktoEXPERT.com
https://www.linkedin.com/in/jweiland
https://www.facebook.com/LinktoEXPERT
https://twitter.com/LinktoEXPERT
www.youtube.com/mylinktoexpert
727.791.7338 phone

JOurneY

Joy Preston

When it comes to career paths, life takes us in many directions. The economy changes, the market changes, supply and demand changes. Even if you have a long-term plan, things can change in an instant and the unexpected may be the best thing to happen.

The 2020 global pandemic may have changed the trajectory of your entire career. You can either fight it or go with it, see where it takes you and try to enjoy the ride. Or you can learn to dance in the rain and wait for the storm to pass. We all have choices to make and we learn to adapt to changes that come. Careers present a moving target, and circumstances can sometimes dictate our paths.

At the end of the nineties, I wanted to plan weddings as my career. Perhaps I thought, because my own wedding would take place in 2000, that I would become an expert and I could plan weddings and events for everyone. In 2001, The Wedding Planner, a movie starring Jennifer Lopez ("J.Lo"), came out. I thought that watching the movie, alone, would provide me with the education and the resources I needed to have a flourishing career in the event industry. I called several venues, using the black tabs of the newspaper, a/k/a "the business section," and found my first hotel job. I enjoyed it and wanted to do it forever—until 9/11 happened and everything changed.

After the attack on the World Trade Center, travel came to a halt and jobs were impacted. Understandably so. It was time to think of other options and put my hospitality-industry career on hold; I would have to place hotels on the back burner for a while. I tried a job in a different industry. Then I found myself back in the hotel world in 2002, when the world was beginning to reopen, working for the Chase Park Plaza (now known as the Chase Park Plaza Royal Sonesta St. Louis).

I found myself working on some amazing events, including my first political event in 2004 as John Kerry was running for president of the United States against George W. Bush. It was my event and I worked with the media, Secret Service, and Kerry's team on this exciting affair. There was a lot to do to make sure everything ran smoothly. And things were changing by the day. As you can imagine, it was a massive production with many factors to consider in planning an event of this magnitude.

The Chase Park Plaza provided great moments and a great opportunity for me because of its historic location and the many special functions they hosted. Its long history and nostalgia made it a fun place to work. Many people wanted to share their memories of proms, weddings, Wrestling at The Chase, and watching their favorite performers in the Khorassan Ballroom. The Chase Park Plaza also included a residential side, which acted as a home for some patients seeking major medical care at Barnes Hospital. I learned so much during my time at this hotel and enjoyed being a part of impactful events.

Another great opportunity I had was working on remarkable events for the Ritz Carlton: events such as Friends of Kids with Cancer, Illumination Gala–The Foundation for Barnes-Jewish Hospital, and extravagant weddings. The staff came from all over the world, bringing with them a wealth of cultural and meaningful knowledge to pull off some one-of-a-kind events. It was hard work and the clients were great.

As 2007 came to an end, the Great Recession hit and the hospitality industry took another major turn. In an instant, things changed and we had to figure out how to keep up with the changes. For many of us in the business, it was time to consider a career change, as staying in a luxury hotel—like flying on a private aircraft—became frowned upon as corporations were forced to lay off personnel and cancel events. Many companies were having to let go of their employees by the hundreds.

I was able to find work in other industries during that time and learned some new skill sets. I also met many people who were in the same boat. Like me, they had trained for one thing for years and had honed in on a single career path, only to have to change direction altogether and start over. Some people realized they enjoyed their new career and were happy that they were forced to make a change. They found that they were a great fit for their new roles and that they could see themselves doing their new jobs for years to come rather than returning to their old jobs when the dust settled. It was eye-opening for so many.

Fast forward to present day—2020/2021 and the global pandemic era. People have had to shift gears, again, and make lemonade out of lemons. Kids have been impacted, as well as employees, teachers, first responders, and pretty much everyone. Students have had to learn how to go to school in a virtual setting and to use their Chromebooks. Teachers have had to learn to teach online, while keeping students engaged and connected. Many have had to learn to work from home in a virtual environment and make the most of it. To avoid public contact, networking groups are now facilitated through Zoom or similar online platforms. Working and networking remotely has allowed us to break down barriers during gatherings that were once held in local coffee shops. Because online meeting sites are virtual platforms, people from other states or countries can attend, expanding participants' networking Rolodexes.

We didn't see the pandemic coming at the beginning of 2020 when the Kansas City Chiefs beat the San Francisco 49ers in the Super Bowl on February 2, 2020. The year had started like any other year; but for many, the Super Bowl was the last major get-together before the world went into lockdown. Major sporting institutions shut down, restaurants closed, and phone apps became more useful than ever. Many people mitigated the risk of being in public by learning to use services, such as Shipt and Instacart, to have groceries and other items delivered on a regular basis. Everyone was affected by the pandemic due to concerns about health, education, and—once again—employment.

The pandemic was a real game changer. People had to learn to adapt, and they had to do it immediately. Many people looked for nuggets of hope and positivity. Actor John Krasinski, from television's The Office, developed a streaming series titled Some Good News to highlight the positive things people were doing all over the world. Upbeat, inspiring news was reported, and Krasinski did a great job of featuring stories with encouraging spins, such as students no longer having a "standard" graduation and medical professionals working twice the hours they did pre-pandemic.

I think we all learned through the pandemic that the only constant is change. Jobs will change and industries will evolve. Software that once was considered efficient in our jobs will be updated to the latest and greatest technology. J.Lo used a headset in The Wedding Planner in 2001; and I have a feeling, had the movie been created in 2021, she could have been Face-Timing with her Apple iPhone due to the advancements in technology.

We've all heard, as technology advances, people may be replaced by computers. Everything changes. There will always be a new idea, a new fad, or a new way of doing things. We have to realize that with change comes meeting new people, facing new adversities, learning new skills, and realizing we may actually be good at something we never set out to achieve. You may have learned you could be forced into something beyond your control, and it may be the best thing yet.

Everyone has the ability to learn new skill sets and see things from a different perspective. We think we are cut out to do one thing because our degree was geared toward a certain job or someone once told us we would be great at something. Our journey makes us unique. We just have to see where it takes us and how we come out on the other side. We all learn from our experiences, peers, and mentors; then we are able to share our experiences with others so they, too, can evolve.

I'm not saying that the pandemic was the best thing that ever happened. I'm saying that it taught us that the sky is the limit with our career choices, and we can try as many things as we want to try. We can all learn from one another and apply what we've learned to the things we do on a regular basis. Our journey is the best part of a career path because it means we are a constant work-in-progress and always willing to make changes and to learn.

Joy Preston is a sales professional and mother of two children.

As a sales professional, Joy has worked in the social and business sectors for large hotels on events, such as weddings, corporate galas, and political and not-for-profit affairs. She also has worked in media and has cultivated great networking groups to team up with business professionals.

Joy is excited to have the opportunity to be a part of the writing world and plans to continue to work on fictional stories in the future.

Joy has a BA in communication with a minor in psychology from Maryville University in St. Louis, Missouri. When Joy is not working, she is spending time with her husband and two children, playing tennis, traveling, watching movies, or reading great books.

Joy can be reached at: scottjoy@juno.com

Cracking the Chrysalis - Surrendering to Transformation

Trish Hall, M.Div.

Cracking the chrysalis is one stage in our individual metamorphosis, a Greek word that means "transformation." It feels like we each wrapped ourselves in a cocoon about March of 2020. We had no idea what was ahead of us. I wonder if, when a caterpillar wraps itself in cozy silk, it understands that the silk is going to harden into a casing, that what it believes itself to be when wrapping will never be the same.

That's rather what happened to us. Like the caterpillar, we released life as we had known it; we dissolved and reformed as something new, or at least we have been offered the opportunity to be a new, best-yet-to-be expression of ourselves.

Cocooning is an interesting behavior, all too familiar for some of us. In early childhood, I withdrew into my cocoon, physically, emotionally, socially, from a hostile household. During the pandemic, some people dropped into old safety nets; others adapted and artfully crafted new ways of being; still others' ineptitude was compounded by confusion arising from disbelief about what was happening, poor leadership, and/or the challenge to separate real from fake news. No one was prepared for "sheltering in place" or news videos of tractor-trailer units lined up by hospitals to receive bodies of those who had perished from the virus—so many bodies that hospital and county morgues could not possibly accommodate them.

In the beginning, it seemed unimaginable that 100,000 people in the US would succumb to the disease. As time went on and the death toll climbed, many became numb to the statistics. The oft-heard phrase was, "It can't go higher"; yet it did, to over 622,000 deaths in the US. How were we to grasp that there would be more than 37 million cases in the US, that businesses would shut down, that schools would close, children would have to be home-schooled by parents, who were similarly unprepared, and then to shift to online learning which didn't work for some because they lost the discipline of routines and supervision? How were we to cope with so many unknowns? We were caught in the swirl of the world—caught in chaos. Despite the torrent of virtual ocean eddies, we could have swum for shore had we figured out where shore was. Many, alas, surrendered to a belief that shore no longer existed. Many, believing themselves to be drowning, gave up and died.

Swift adaptations enabled select individuals to learn how to swim in the new waters—some profiteered. Some grabbed for water wings to create the illusion that they were able to swim. Much like trying to submerge a beach ball, eventually illusions pop to the surface and burst. Overwhelm that had been stuffed down erupted more horrifically than if it had been addressed from the onset. Our survival instinct pushed us to make sense out of whatever was going on— to reconcile chaos. We demonstrated insanity by trying to reason with what was totally unreasonable.

Considering the many changes in our external circumstances, it was encouraging to observe creative resilience and adaptability. We crafted new ways of being, leaning into change and making it work. We witnessed what had changed and revealed new strategies to accommodate; we became safe harbors and provided paths through the maze and out the far side.

Although some of us may have felt like our natural circadian rhythm had time-warped into a cicada's seventeen-year cycle, the time had come to break out of our chrysalis, to venture into being physically, socially engaged. The prospect of "re-entry" was not a universally shared experience. Disquieting, if not outright alarming, to those who had hunkered down in the predictability of life in a cocoon; stifling to those pining for physical connection.

The progress with vaccines stirred newfound courage among many and caused resistance in others. As the country was beginning to wake up, word of virulent variants around the world, and then here in the United States, sent shockwaves of fear—fear of the virus, but even more, fear of another shutdown surged. Some international borders re-closed. Thoughts of "Dare I break out of my cozy chrysalis" arose. Nature nudged, "It's time." Fear said, "Not yet." Rebirth was underway. I wondered what the butterfly feels as it becomes stronger with each push in its struggle to be free. It knows it cannot turn back—forward is the only available direction.

So what is the difference between those who succumbed to overwhelm and those who strode through virtually unscathed yet forever different? Resilience, non-egocentricity, consciously chosen strategies, the willingness to release attachment to what was known and the faith to take the next step with no assurance that it would be the right step. Interestingly, the willingness to take that next step on faith drastically shifted the odds that it was the right step.

The prospect of being free, back out in the world, was both thrilling and intimidating to me. Will anything feel familiar? How am I to be? Doubt and its companion, fear, raised their ugly heads. Do I have the courage to emerge from the safety of my cocoon? How would thriving in my cocoon translate to shedding its shield? I confronted myself, cleared out cobwebs, and took inventory. Who am I in this new iteration?

Two, simultaneous, elements emerged. I had to:

✓ Stop living "subject to" circumstances and the opinions of others

✓ Live the truth of what I am, embodying Spirit expressing as me

Transformation, a thorough or dramatic change in the form, appearance, or character, is our metamorphosis—the dropping away of what was known in order to awaken to whatever is, is not for the faint of heart. The willingness to transform is the ultimate declaration of faith. We must let go of what we know—all those reassuring identifiers—to make space to be alive as Spirit. Beyond beliefs that often rely on conditions for validation, Spiritual transformation calls us to surrender to a new incarnation outside our prior inkling. This is the declaration, "Here I am, Lord. Use me!" without checking it out in advance to see if it is an assignment that meets our worldly concept of ourselves. The resulting freedom restores clarity, revealing a simplicity that can thrive within chaos.

Always dedicated to peace, love and compassion, I began to question my "whys." Challenged by inner dialogue, "Are my gifts good enough?" "Am I good enough?" Had I permitted those doubts to corrupt the quality of my gifts? Had I been giving freely or bartering—unconsciously seeking something in return?

Rather than a call to reinvent myself or make temporary changes to fit with others more easily, my metamorphosis was the call to re-align with my "divine prototype," to tune into being the values and qualities that make this human experience the gift. Laid open as a Spiritual Being, a question arose, "Am I granting myself unconditional high regard? Do I love myself?" I realized I loved Spirit as me, yet I did not extend that unconditionality to my human self. I had separated myself into two co-existing entities: Spirit and human, sharing one body. I had to reclaim my wholeness: Spirit in expression *AS me, not with me.* This was a giant step in re-unifying myself—a key to not only surviving but actually thriving as a result of the pandemic.

I recommitted to sitting in the stillness every day, long enough to discern how I am to be and drawing on the wisdom of the stillness when challenges present themselves—then I calmly choose how to respond, confident that circumstances are not in control; I control how I relate to circumstances.

I re-examined my relationship with myself. Knowing all that I know about my humanity, I asked, "Am I able to accept and love myself—all of myself— without conditions?" I was relieved when the response from deep inside was a congruent, affirmative "Yes!" Had it been hesitant, I know that Spirit within would have called me to dive deeper, to reveal what prompted the hesitancy. Shift was happening.

I rededicated myself to do my part to create a world that works for everyone—one in which all creation is honored, and each person is seen, heard, and valued—fostering Infinity Groups in which we learn from one another about how it is to be in the ever-changing contemporary world from their perspective, generating a ripple effect of compassion and connection, touching and transforming the lives of countless others around the planet.

Although I don't know anyone who has declared, "Wow! Can we do this all again?" I look at the personal and spiritual growth that has occurred and am grateful for the pandemic journey—even amid the grief that one of our sons-in-law was an early covid death.

The key to how I found my way through my metamorphosis is so simple. I remembered to live the truth of what I am: Spirit in expression as me. Truly a metamorphosis. The rewards are exhilarating!

Therisia "Trish" Hall, M.Div., is an insightful international best-selling author, speaker, and coach, who blends wisdom, authenticity, humor, and compassion in furtherance of her passion-conscious inclusivity.

Whether addressing audiences, facilitating communication among diverse populations, working with students or individual clients, she thrives on awakening the unique magnificence within each, empowering all to live their "best yet to be."

Drawing on experiences as a student of life, in myriad world settings, Trish uses her innate ability to recognize commonalities to enhance connections among diverse populations that birthed Way2Peace, a foundation dedicated to honoring the dignity of all life.

Trish, an outstanding educator, facilitator, consultant and mediator, founded The Training Source, specialists in interpersonal and organizational communication, which serves government and private sector, non-profits and for-profits.

Trish is a master practitioner and trainer of NLP certified in Ericksonian Hypnosis, a certified practitioner of Interactive Imagery Therapy, a bereavement counselor, and meditation teacher.

Trishhall.unltd@gmail.com
www.linkedin.com/in/trish-hall-3898016/
trish.way2peace@gmail.com
www.way2peace.org
www.cslmetro.org
revtrish.cslmetro@gmail.com

What's My WHY?

Dr. Jennifer Martin

As a teen, the chaos that surrounded my health led me down the path of my healing journey. This path brought me to a place of clarity, helping me to find my purpose and identify my "WHY." On that journey, I learned that we are all gifted with talents that are meant to be shared with the world.

While I was working on my healing journey, I realized that helping others would be my gift to the world. I was eager to help and support others so that they, too, could reclaim their power and live their best lives. Remember, when you are amid pain and struggling, be patient, give yourself grace. This will help to bring you clarity. The opening of your gift is often right on the other side of your struggle.

At the age of thirteen, my chiropractor diagnosed me with hypoglycemia. I had suffered through a chaotic year-long search for answers as to why I was experiencing debilitating symptoms, such as almost passing out, shaking, extreme fatigue, irregular or fast heartbeat, paleness, sweating, numbness, and tingling, with occasional lightheadedness, spaciness, dizziness, inability to stay focused or think clearly, and blurry vision. I had seen several different specialists. None of them knew what was wrong with me because, in hindsight, none of them performed the correct multi-hour glucose tolerance test that my chiropractor did. I am grateful to my parents for their ongoing search and determination to never give up.

One Saturday morning, while getting my wellness adjustment, my chiropractor asked me, "Is there anything else I can help you with?" Out of desperation, my mom began to explain my worsening symptoms. I had been fasting that morning, so he could test me over the next three hours, but, likely, he said, I had hypoglycemia.

The chiropractor drew baseline blood work and then had me drink an orange-flavored glucose solution. For the first time in over a year, I didn't feel loopy and spacy. My hand looked like it was attached to my body, as strange as that sounds. He checked my blood sugar every hour during the test, which, on the first review, spiked high. Upon rechecking the next hour, it began to drop. After my third-hour blood draw, he stopped the test because my blood sugar was so low. I was about to pass out and could barely put a sentence together. The test confirmed: Hypoglycemia. Finally, I had answers and some clarity to the constant state of chaotic survival mode I had mentally and physically been living in.

Hypoglycemia causes blood sugar (glucose) levels to be lower than normal. Glucose is the body and brain's primary energy source. When blood glucose levels drop below seventy to eighty milligrams per deciliter, hypoglycemic warning symptoms begin. At this stage, panic and anxiety may also occur.

As fate would have it, the chiropractor's wife also had hypoglycemia. That afternoon, they took my family and me under their wings and taught us the tools that would help me be successful in overcoming my symptoms. They coached me to eat small meals and snacks spread out throughout the day, every two to three hours. My food choices had to include three things: a complex carbohydrate to bring my sugar level back up when it was starting to drop, minimal fat source and protein to help stabilize my sugar level longer. I could eat low glycemic fruits and vegetables that had high fiber with proteins and fats. I had to avoid high glycemic fruits, veggies, and unnaturally sweetened fruit juices unless I had a low blood-sugar episode. Then I would use high-glycemic foods or drinks to get my sugar level up quickly.

I drank plenty of water and avoided caffeine, since caffeine intake could mimic my hypoglycemic symptoms. I wasn't interested in going to parties or hanging out with big groups of kids, since I couldn't eat pizza, chips, doughnuts, and soda. Alcohol was out of the question.

I felt isolated, depressed, and lonely during most of my three-year healing journey. I was blessed to be surrounded by family, mentors, and close friends. Their love and support helped me focus on myself and empowered me to keep my eye on my long-term success.

I was an active kid and started dancing and doing gymnastics at the age of three. Over time, I also played various sports. During my childhood, my family ate healthy. However, while my extracurricular and after-school activities continued to increase, sometimes four to five hours a night, my healthy eating habits started to diminish. Skipped meals, microwavable dinners, and fast-food drive-throughs in the car to and from cheerleading and dance class were burning my body out physically. This fast-paced lifestyle may have contributed to my hypoglycemia since it didn't run in my family.

During my health journey, proper food choices, more frequent meals/snacks, and decreasing my activity were helping, but unpredictable symptoms, such as anxiety and fear, began to develop. At times, when my glucose levels went too low, my body would go into fight or flight mode and cause panic and anxiety symptoms. Those symptoms were just as bad some days as the hypoglycemia itself. At times, my life felt like an uncontrollable roller coaster. I quickly realized I needed mindset support as well as physical support. I chose to be on anti-anxiety medication for about a year while I learned to implement other treatment methods to help support me. The medication was a great transition tool for me and helped me stay calmer when I wasn't in control of my anxiety flair-ups.

I learned to rely on blood-glucose monitoring, biofeedback stickers, NLP, tapping, breathing techniques, and listening to relaxation/meditation tapes at bedtime and in the moments when my mind and anxiety were racing. Through utilizing these tools, I learned to differentiate true hypoglycemic symptoms from panic and anxiety symptoms.

By implementing proper nutrition, balancing my activity level, and utilizing mindset tools, I began to heal. Within two years, I started golfing, running track, doing gymnastics, and dancing again. After three years of strict discipline, grit, and determination, the uncertainty of hypoglycemia no longer controlled me. I was finally able to lead a more normal life.

By age nineteen, I could eat an expanded food palate but preferred to stick to healthy eating and drinking water. I could have nothing with added unnatural sugar, high fat, or high sodium content, with little to no added preservatives if possible. My body craved healthy eating, providing me with long-term sustainable energy. My skin glowed; I felt more stable; and I maintained my ideal weight. I learned to read nutrition labels and prepare weekly meal/snack plans utilizing healthy cooking techniques. These were key to my long-term success.

Looking back at age thirteen when it all began, I had so much responsibility for my own body and health. Today, I can sit in a place of peace and acceptance when I reflect on the years that I struggled with my health. I have gratitude for how it has shaped the rest of my life. I gained the clarity of realizing why I had endured my suffering. It ignited a strong desire in me to help coach others through their own healing journey.

When I look around in our world today, I see many people struggling—some physically, some emotionally, and far too many silently. I want them to know there is hope and people who care.

Don't endure it alone. There are professionals to guide you, give you answers, and provide implementable solutions through your healing journey.

Research has found a biopsychosocial approach is the best model of health/wellness care. It is an interdisciplinary model that utilizes the interconnection of care between biology, psychology, and socio-environmental factors to maximize clinical outcomes and lasting results for patients. It allows for providers and patient-support networks around them to look at their available resources for the most comprehensive and implementable treatment plans. Patients must also be willing to create a positive, nourishing environment that helps them thrive and partner with their providers by giving honest feedback and data reporting for the best clinical outcomes as I was able to achieve on my journey.

I am passionate about teaching others the skills and tools needed to heal, while supporting them in their journey. I survived my chaotic health crisis as a teen and, through that, I learned that the greatest gift you can give someone is the GIFT of THEMSELVES!

Please don't give up on yourself or others. Everyone and everything are puzzle pieces in the larger picture of your life. Keep pushing through and searching for the next piece to put into place in your puzzle.

I began college at the age of sixteen. I was ready to start my journey to become a doctor and healer with the resounding life purpose of helping others. To this day, I feel so blessed to have the opportunity to be that gift in people's lives. It is my passion and great joy to have realized my WHY—to help inspire others to create a healthier and happier life.

Dr. Jennifer Martin holds a doctor of chiropractic degree and a bachelor of science specializing in human anatomy and physiology. As a certified ergonomic assessment specialist, she provides solutions for the prevention of workplace injuries. She has completed postgraduate training in sports rehabilitation, scoliosis, minimally invasive spine surgery, nutrition, pregnancy, pediatrics, spectrum disorders, and acupuncture.

Dr. Martin is founder and CEO of Healthy Community Group. Her company has helped educate and develop implementable plans to support thousands of women and families through their health journeys. Her team of experts incorporate five key elements, including body, mindset, image, nutrition, and community, to help clients execute their healthy weight and life goals.

Dr. Martin is passionate about supporting various not-for-profit groups that coach children and families to live healthier, active lives. Through her company, she feels blessed to be a gift to others by helping them achieve a healthy lifestyle for life.

Dr. Jennifer Martin DC, CEAS
www.drjennmartin.com
drjennhcgroup@gmail.com

Letting Go with Gratitude

Lisa Jean Dickmann, M.A.

"God, I give You my life. What do You want me to do with it?"

I ask this question at turning points in my life. But this time, it was different. I felt clearly called, called to help others tidy their spaces. It's laughable because my own home wasn't tidy! For years I had tried and failed to get it tidy. And was there even such a job as a tidying coach? Regardless, it was my calling. And I ignored it! Instead, I applied for a job doing something unrelated, didn't get the job, but did get pregnant, and finally—months later—I answered the call.

I signed up for a training course that would take me to Chicago over an extended weekend to prepare me to start a business as a tidying consultant. I also bought the domain "tidyupgrade.com," and *finally* got my home tidy.

I never succeeded in tidying my home until finding a book called *The Life-Changing Magic of Tidying Up*.[1] To say tidying changed my life is an understatement; my life was totally transformed. Through the pages of the book, author Marie Kondo taught me to tidy using my intuition. I learned that tidying is actually a simple process with just two decisions: what to keep, and where to put the things I kept. I touched each possession I owned, asking if it sparked joy, as Kondo instructed. If I loved something, I kept it; if I didn't, it felt heavy, like I was being weighed down, and I got rid of it. Before letting an item go, I said, "thank you," and let it go with gratitude in my heart. I discovered that gratitude lays the foundation for joy.

Tidying, like grief, is a process of letting go. Through this whole-hearted process, we create clarity out of chaos and make space for joy.

---

[1] Marie Kondo and Cathy Hiranoi. The Life-Changing Magic of Tidying Up: The Japanese Art of Decluttering and Organizing. 1st American ed., Berkley: Ten Speed Press, 2014.

After I had tidied my clothes, I filled newly emptied drawers with baby clothes for the little girl we were expecting in a few short months. Trusting my intuition created space for joy. I felt thrilled! Little did I know that the moment I put everything in place, all the pieces would fall out from under me.

Before leaving for our road trip to Chicago, where I'd learn to help others declutter and organize their homes, my house was as tidy as it had ever been. Twenty-nine weeks pregnant, with my perfectly packed suitcase, my husband, and our three young children, we set out. We were halfway to Chicago when my phone rang. My ob-gyn was calling with a diagnosis for our unborn child. It was the moment that joy left my life.

"The test results are consistent with a diagnosis of Trisomy 18. Your baby has three copies of her eighteenth chromosome instead of the usual two." Continuing, he explained that our daughter was medically unstable and severely disabled. He imparted grim statistics, including a fifty percent chance of stillbirth. And if she was born alive, he relayed heartbreaking odds of celebrating a first birthday—just ten percent.

Crushed, I could hardly catch my breath. All my excitement and joy about the Chicago seminar, my tidy house, my expected baby girl, and my plan to start an organizing business disappeared instantly. Filled with grief, tears poured from my eyes until we got to the Chicago hotel, where my husband took the kids to the pool. Alone in the room, I cried out to God, asking why He would do this. Why would He take my baby? It was the darkest moment of my life.

I kept going. The next day, arriving at the seminar in a haze, I felt positive energy radiating throughout the room. I put on a smile and immersed myself in the excitement and joy of the other organizers-in-training. In the midst of my newfound grief, that day I found myself in one of the happiest places on earth. The hand of God had led me to this place at this time. I could not have orchestrated it more perfectly.

In the evening, I returned to the hotel room and again fell to pieces, overwhelmed by grief and shock. My baby was dying. And there was nothing I could do about it. I fell asleep after reading inspiring stories of families of Trisomy 18 children. I awoke at two a.m. with a new feeling: Gratitude. I suddenly felt incredibly strong and well-prepared to confront this challenge, like when I had confronted my possessions. Overwhelmed by gratitude, I felt...

▲ Grateful for the twenty-nine weeks I had already had with this baby.

▲ Grateful for learning her diagnosis early enough to mentally and emotionally prepare for the uncertain journey ahead.

▲ Grateful for every loving kick the baby gave me, showing that she was alive and strong.

▲ Grateful that I was with my husband and not alone in Chicago.

▲ Grateful that I was immersed in a joy-filled environment at the seminar.

▲ Grateful for my intent to start a business helping people tidy and experience more joy.

▲ Grateful that starting this business would be a positive force in my life during a very difficult time.

▲ Grateful for my faith, which gave me extra strength during this time of crisis.

▲ Grateful for the gift of this special child and this unique journey.

Later that day, I shared my new-found gratitude face-to-face with author Marie Kondo. My heart overflowing, I expressed my deep thanks for teaching me how to tidy and creating this method that brought me to a joy-filled place when I needed it most. I knew that her teachings would continue to support me through the difficult journey ahead.

Ten weeks later, my sweet baby, Cecelia Faith, passed away at birth. Letting go of possessions was easy by comparison. Consumed with grief, the baby clothes I'd put in my drawers did not delight my broken heart. They weighed me down! I pulled the clothes from my drawers, stuffed them into a box, and stashed them in the basement. To get through this difficult time, I relied on the simple habits that kept my home tidy, like doing laundry, washing dishes, and putting things back where they belonged, with appreciation in my heart.

When people die, they leave their things behind. Because Cecelia left this world so soon, she had not had time to acquire belongings or wear the baby clothes I had packed away. She did, however, wear one beautiful dress, hand-knitted especially for her and truly worthy of how special she was. Would the dress make my heart leap with joy? I held it in my hands... No, I didn't feel joy, but I did not feel weighed down either. I felt love. So much love. That's what they say about grief: It is love with no place to go. I kept the dress, but letting go of Cecelia was the hardest thing I have ever done; and I knew, after her death and letting her go, I could let go of anything. Possessions would never be as important as the people I love.

I waited until Cecelia's first birthday before I revisited the box of baby clothes in the basement. At that point, I was fortunate to be expecting another baby, due in three months. Our ultrasound revealed that not only was our new baby healthy and whole, it was also undeniably a boy! I would not be needing the baby girl clothes for him and passed them on to another bereaved mother who was about to deliver a little girl. I felt joy, blessed even, to be able to give these clothes to her. The blessings continued with the arrival of our son, healthy and handsome. He brings pure delight to our home every day.

When you go through heartbreak, remember that, like a seed, the heart must break open in order to grow. Work to become the best version of yourself and choose to live joyfully, even when it's difficult. Gratitude and love build a foundation for joy that is only possible with an open heart. When you are grateful every day for what you have, your heart will fill with love.

Throughout the diagnosis and subsequent death of my daughter, I chose to live joyfully with gratitude for the journey that opened my heart to grow in ways that it never could have without the heartbreak. Every day with my son is a gift that I wouldn't have without Cecelia. I am now able to walk with others through their grief with greater compassion and understanding, as I help them let go with gratitude.

What do you need to let go of to make space for joy?

Takeaways when tidying:

▲ Tidying is a healing process that requires vulnerability.

▲ Enlist the support of a friend or professional.

▲ Use Marie Kondo's question: "Does it spark joy?"

▲ Connect with your intuition and be honest with yourself.

▲ Let go quickly and with sincere gratitude.

Gratitude lays the foundation for joy.
Lisa Jean Dickmann

Recognizing the value of listening skills and empathy, Lisa Jean Dickmann earned a master's degree in counseling. After becoming a mom, she wanted a solution to the clutter in her home. Tidying led Lisa to discover her true mission in life. Lisa became Missouri's first certified KonMari Consultant in 2017 and found her counseling skills to be the perfect fit.

Lisa focuses her organizing business, Tidy Upgrade, on helping people make space for what matters most by letting go with gratitude. These transformations enable her clients to flourish and live in alignment with their dreams. Lisa sees clients in-person, virtually, and she offers speaking engagements that inspire audiences to tidy up. Remember, when you tidy your home, you upgrade your life!

Lisa lives life joyfully in St. Louis with her husband and four children, ages three to thirteen.

lisa@tidyupgrade.com
https://tidyupgrade.com
https://instagram.com/tidyupgrade
https://facebook.com/tidyupgrade

Faith as a Foundation for Clarity

Marie Chewe-Elliott, M.A.

Do you know what it feels like to walk in the dark? I've done it many times in my home and also in my faith journey.

Here's how it goes: The lights are off. I can't see the furniture, ceiling, or walls, but I know they are still there. I can't see the floor, but I can feel it holding me up. I trust that it can sustain me, even if I misstep, and it gives me the confidence to keep moving forward. This is parallel to my faith journey.

I first recall walking in what felt like some supernatural, slow-motion darkness during my unplanned pregnancy, marriage, and subsequent divorce, before I even left for undergraduate school. It was bad enough to get pregnant in my small Bible-belt town, but I also dared to recognize this marriage was wrong for me (*and my baby*) and divorced. Talk about walking in the dark.

Like the floor provides my stability when I walk through the dark house, faith was then and continues to be the foundation that holds me together and propels me to move forward. Having spent every Sunday of my life in a Baptist church as a youngster, I had heard a few things that I believed with all my heart. Among those teachings were that Jesus died for *ME*, powerful scriptures like John 3:16 and Romans 8:28, and that God would forgive my missteps!! I learned about the great icons of faith, such as Abraham, David, Esther, and others. More importantly, I learned about the "saints" right in my congregation. I watched women and men with less-than-ideal family and home situations pray, worship, and serve faithfully. I watched them worship after losing a child or spouse. I watched them hold onto faith while dealing with an incarcerated spouse or an addicted child.

Surviving my experience of pregnancy and the birth of my beautiful baby boy was pivotal to my life's direction. It marked the start of the purposeful and intentional growth in my faith walk. I shed anyone and anything that didn't align with my journey. That was the first time I recall stepping out on faith with literally nothing but a prayer. But it would not be the last.

Over the years, faith has helped me navigate the various twists and turns of life. Without faith, I certainly couldn't have dreamed of the thirtieth anniversary my husband and I just celebrated. By faith, we raised the children, faced health challenges, earned advanced academic degrees, assisted aging parents, and made the best of job changes—now, we can add civil unrest, political animosity, and a global pandemic. The conditions are ripe for chaos and darkness on any given day.

The notable saints in Hebrews 11 (Enoch, Abraham, Noah, et cetera) demonstrate that the power and breadth of faith are vast and appropriate in any situation.

Faith has undoubtedly guided me to the best days and through the worst days of my life. It has compelled me to leave some places where my heart wanted to stay. It has repelled my fear and given me strength. Faith has provided clarity and light in my darkest hour. I have sometimes reflected on some of these trials and declared the words from an old gospel song that states, "My soul looks back and wonders how I got over..." As I have matured, spiritually (and chronologically), I know at least one of the answers to how I've kept from losing my mind amid crisis and chaos is simply FAITH. It remains the foundation to clarity in every situation of my life.

I am learning to approach crises by doing what I call "faithing my way through." Romans 4:11 states that God can speak things that don't exist into existence. "Faithing" requires that I trust His power and promises for my life. If I am sick, I claim my healing. If I am sad, I celebrate joy. If I am mad, I look for reasons to be glad. I pray over whatever it is, lean into grace and accept that the answer may be to move forward or be still.

As I write this, my husband is preparing for surgery. Although it is my preference that he did not need this procedure, that is not reality. So I have some choices. I can throw a pity party and be in a state of doom and gloom. I can be in denial. Or I can choose to approach this based on my faith experience. That experience tells me that whatever the outcome, my faith will sustain me, as it always has.

Women of Faith
(Proverbs 31:10-31, Ephesians 6:10-19, Titus 2:3-5)

As a little girl growing up in a small Baptist church in Mississippi, I loved and revered the pastor and respected the deacons; but I wanted to BE those dynamic church ladies. Women like my mother and grandmothers—those praying, tarrying, hat-wearing, Bible-carrying, women. We called them the church mothers or Mothers' Board back then. As an adult, I learned they were living examples of the women in Proverbs 31 and Titus 2. Now, I call them "women of faith." I celebrate and honor them with this poem, and I'm still trying to be like them.

Women of faith love the unlovable, see the invisible, feel the
    intangible and with God's help we do the impossible every day.
Women of faith press our way through the crowd and as the Spirit moves
    we sometimes lift our hands and praise out loud.
Women of faith put down pettiness, jealousy, and insecurity and
    put on the belt of truth, the breastplate of righteousness,
    shield of faith, the helmet of salvation, and sword of the Spirit.
Women of faith must get healed, delivered and set free
    while chauffeuring children, cooking meals and buying groceries.
It is a fact that we can do more in two hours than most folks
    do all day.
We are moms, wives, daughters, grannies, and aunties.
AND entrepreneurs, teachers, preachers, nurses—you name it!
Women of faith cannot be deterred by errant spouses, disobedient
    children, threat of war, tragedy, diseases, uprisings, or downsizings.
Regardless of what's going on in the world women of faith keep marching
    on, keep praying and keep on saying that "Jesus is Lord."
Women of faith accept nothing that gets in our way.
We don't fall out, give in or give up.
Women of faith—God's women—
Stand up and keep on keeping the faith!

Marie Chewe-Elliott

Yvonne

Marie Chewe-Elliott is a writer, speaker, and poet in north St. Louis County.

She is the author of three books of poetry and a children's book. Her poems have been published in The St. Louis Anthology, *SO Magazine*, *St. Louis Writers Guild Anthology*, UMSL's *Litmag*, and among winning selections in the 2019 Arts Rolla Writing Competition and Arts in Transit's 2019 Metro Lines Contest. In 2012, she cofounded North County Writing & Arts Network.

Marie's love of words guided her to a career of more than thirty years in various facets of communication, including newspaper reporter, nonprofit and government communications, and adjunct lecturer.

Marie earned degrees from the University of Mississippi and Webster University.

Connect with Marie at:
myelliott61@gmail.com
Facebook, Instagram and Clubhouse

314-210-4774 Cell

NOW is the TIME to be VISIBLE, CREDIBLE, and UNFORGETTABLE

**You've been thinking about writing a book . . .
but not sure where to start?**

Start with <u>ONE</u> chapter
in a professionally produced Anthology!

Collaborate, Connect, and Celebrate!

- Collaborate with your co-authors and reduce
  your publishing expenses by 90%!

- Connect with your co-authors and introduce your
  business to hundreds, if not thousands, of new prospects!

- Celebrate your accomplishments, as you participate
  in a global marketing campaign and become an
  Amazon Bestselling Author!

Contact **cathy@daviscreative.com** to
reserve your chapter in our next anthology.

Made in the USA
Monee, IL
02 November 2021